POWERFUL READERS

Thinking Strategies to Guide Literacy Instruction in Secondary Classrooms

KYLA HADDEN

ADRIENNE GEAR

Pembroke Publishers Limited

© 2016 Pembroke Publishers
538 Hood Road
Markham, Ontario, Canada L3R 3K9
www.pembrokepublishers.com

Distributed in the U.S. by Stenhouse Publishers
480 Congress Street
Portland, ME 04101
www.stenhouse.com

Library and Archives Canada Cataloguing in Publication

Hadden, Kyla, author
    Powerful readers: thinking strategies to guide literacy instruction in secondary classrooms / Kyla Hadden, Adrienne Gear.

Issued in print and electronic formats.
ISBN 978-1-55138-313-2 (paperback).--ISBN 978-1-55138-919-6 (pdf)

    1. Reading comprehension. 2. Reading (Secondary). I. Gear, Adrienne, author II. Title.

LB1632.H33 2016   428.4071'2   C2016-903256-6
                                             C2016-903257-4

Editor: Kat Mototsune
Cover Design: John Zehethofer
Typesetting: Jay Tee Graphics Ltd.

Printed and bound in Canada
9 8 7 6 5 4 3 2 1

FSC
www.fsc.org
MIX
Paper from
responsible sources
FSC® C004071

Contents

Foreword

So often, over the years, I have heard high-school teachers say that it is not their job to teach reading and that students coming to their classes should already know how to read. What they may not understand is that there is a huge difference between decoding and understanding; while many of their students are able to decode, many might not understand what they are reading. What is often disregarded is that there is a huge difference between *doing* reading and *teaching* reading, that "assigning and assessing" comprehension questions at the back of a chapter is not enhancing students' understanding of the text they are reading. In order for students to fully comprehend a text, teachers need to go beyond a literal understanding and learn how to think through and beyond that text: to make connections to themselves and other texts; to question and infer; to visualize and synthesize. Senior-secondary teacher Kyla Hadden understands all of these things about reading, about thinking, and about learning. Not only does she understand this, but she uses this knowledge as the foundation upon which she designs and implements her senior-secondary English classes. And now she is committed to helping every high-school English and content-area teacher understand it, too. And so she felt compelled to write this book.

I first met Kyla several years ago when I was leading a Reading Power leadership team with middle-school teachers in Salmon Arm, B.C. I was concerned when I saw her name on the attendance list the first day because she identified herself as a *Sr. English teacher*. Coming from an elementary-level teaching background, I expressed my concern to the Director of Instruction, Wendy Woodhurst, that Kyla might not find the learning very relevant to her practice. Wendy responded, "Don't worry. Kyla is a master teacher. She will adapt!" Well, in a very short time, I came to realize that Wendy was absolutely right—Kyla is a master teacher. Each lesson I shared, Kyla took and adapted for her Senior English classes. I was always excited to see the lessons Kyla did with her students when we broke into sharing circles. Week after week, I was blown away by the amazing, creative lessons she taught her Grade 11 and 12 students. I loved how she used authentic literature and picture books to teach the strategies with her older students. I loved that she seemed to create a natural community of learners within her classroom, so that students felt comfortable sharing their thinking and learning with her and with each other. I loved how she challenged their thinking throughout her lessons. I loved when she told me that Reading Power was something she knew had been missing in her instruction and that she would never go back to teaching without it.

Meaningful learning—this is why we teach. This is why we strive to make our teaching practice more effective every day, every week, every year. Kyla Hadden is a teacher who strives to make learning meaningful for her high-school students. Kyla believes all students are capable of reading more thoughtfully and knows that it is through explicit and intentional teaching that they can reach their full potential. She is creative, innovative, inspiring, and a born teacher. Because she is a practicing teacher, the lessons in this book are authentic and explained as clear, step-by-step instructions. She outlines the strategies for both fiction and nonfiction reading with practical lessons and reproducible templates that can easily be integrated into any high-school English classroom. She recommends literature, poetry, and picture books that she has used in her classes to model and teach the lessons, and she provides rubrics for each of the fiction and nonfiction reading powers.

I am thrilled to be part of this book and to know that the work teachers have been doing to make learning, reading, and thinking better for their students in elementary and middle schools is now moving into secondary schools. I am grateful to Kyla for her willingness to take a risk, to think outside the box, and to be the voice of secondary teachers raising the level of expectations for their students and challenging them to read and think deeply and thoughtfully into the world.

— Adrienne Gear

Introduction

When I started my teaching career, I found that my education had given me very little knowledge about how people learned to read and write. I came out of university with a good understanding of how to plan lessons and units, but with little understanding of the purpose behind those lessons and units. Luckily, I was teaching older students who already knew how to read and write. Or at least that was what I thought. Boy, was I wrong! While many of my students were able to decode words and gain literal understanding while reading, they really weren't thinking about what they were reading. Also, while many of my students could spell words and form sentences and paragraphs, their writing was often mundane and unfocused. Most of my students had acquired good literacy building blocks, but they lacked the knowledge to construct anything meaningful with these building blocks.

When I think back to my first few years of teaching, I want to apologize to my students. While we did a lot of interesting activities and assignments, I didn't explicitly teach them anything about reading or writing. I taught them the way I was taught in high school: I assigned things to be read with questions and activities to be answered and completed; I assigned essays and stories and poems to be written. Those who already "got it" were fine. Those who knew how to read and write well continued to do so. However, those who didn't read and write well also continued to do so.

When students would read and tell me that they didn't get it or couldn't find the information, my most common response was to tell them to read it again. I wrongly believed that students would understand what they were reading if they just focused and read it a few times. I knew they could decode the words and, in my mind, that meant they could understand it.

My writing instruction consisted of showing students how to organize their writing for the assigned task, followed by giving proofreading time to fix their mistakes. The focus for proofreading was spelling and grammar. I spent little time on teaching students how to improve their writing or how to communicate effectively. This "assign and assess" pattern, as Richard Allington (2002) calls it, has little benefit for those who have not already acquired the skill that is the focus of the assignment.

I was first introduced to Adrienne Gear's Reading Power when I was invited by an administrator to attend a series of workshops being given in my school district. She wasn't sure how much I would get out of the workshops for my own classroom, since they were directed at elementary teachers, but hoped that they could help bridge the gap between what was happening around literacy in elementary schools and what was happening (or not happening) around literacy in secondary schools.

That first series of workshops changed me as a teacher. I heard from elementary teachers who were trying to teach their students the same skills I was asking my students to use in secondary school. They wanted to help their students learn skills like connecting and inferring—I was asking my students to connect and infer. As I read through the first edition of Adrienne's book, *Reading Power*, I used the sequential nature of the lessons in developing my own lessons to explicitly teach the powers to my high-school students. I focused on modeling the strategies, allowed students opportunities to practice the powers, and finally had them use the powers independently.

At the end of that first school year, I sat down to mark the written literary response portion of the final exam with a colleague. We noticed that, in their responses, students were actually using the language we had taught them. They were able to communicate their connections and inferences. Most were able to see beyond the literal meaning of the texts they were required to read as part of the exam. From that point on, I knew that Reading Power, with its explicit instruction, needed to be a part of literacy instruction at the middle- and high-school levels.

I continued to attend all workshops offered by Adrienne Gear in my local area. I am not ashamed to admit that I became a bit of a groupie! When Adrienne published *Nonfiction Reading Power*, I quickly incorporated the nonfiction powers into both my English and content-area classes. I did the same when she released the Writing Power books. Because of this, I believe that I have been able to help my students become powerful readers and writers.

This book is designed to help teachers develop an effective reading and writing program in their high-school classrooms. I try to provide a balance of theory and practical lessons. I provide information on organizing your year or semester; note that these are just suggestions that I found have worked for me. I firmly believe that there is no such thing as one best practice when it comes to teaching; instead, there are many different forms of "wise practice" that work for individual teachers and their students. We know that "good teachers, effective teachers, manage to produce better achievement regardless of which curriculum materials, pedagogical approach, or reading program is selected" (Allington, 2002). It is my hope that you take these ideas and make them work for you, your classroom, and your students.

The book starts with an overview of using Reading Power in the classroom, including the basics of the Reading Power approach, information on organizing literacy instruction in classrooms, and thoughts on moving literacy instruction outside the traditional blocks that form the basis of most middle- and secondary-school timetables. Part A shows how to teach and use Reading Power for fiction, covering the reading powers of Connecting, Visualizing, Questioning, Inferring, and Transforming; these chapters include a focus on a literary device and suggested texts to support the lessons, as well as a rubric for each strategy. Part B shows how to teach and use Reading Power with nonfiction, covering the reading powers of Questioning, Zooming In, Determining Importance, Questioning/Inferring, and Transforming/Synthesizing; these chapters include curricular connections to different subjects and a rubric for each nonfiction reading power.

1   Welcome to Powerful Reading

I grew up in a household of readers. Almost every Saturday, my family would head into town and drive straight to the used bookstore. There we would trade in the books that we were finished with for new treasures for the week ahead. Having always been a voracious reader, I never quite understood when people (both students and adults) told me that they didn't enjoy reading. How could you not be carried away into the imaginary world of a good book or story? How could you not connect to the experiences of a great character? Maybe they just hadn't found the right book or story yet. And it caused me physical pain when people read one of my favorite texts and told me that they didn't enjoy it. How could they not love that book? It never occurred to me that the reader contributes to the story, enabling different readers to come to different understandings and appreciation of the text.

Finally, my discovery of Adrienne Gear's Reading Power gave me the language to describe the things that were happening in my head when I was reading. I now had the language to use with students in my classroom. In the beginning of my career, before Reading Power, my classroom discussions were dominated by me and the students who "got it" and were already good readers. The other students stared blankly when asked questions that went beyond the literal meaning of a text. With Reading Power, I found I could model my thinking to all of my students. I could teach them the language to communicate their thinking about what they are reading.

What Makes a Powerful Reader?

Reading Strategies

The Reading Power strategies were developed from the research of a man named David Pearson. While working as a professor at the University of Michigan in the 1970s, Pearson set out to discover what made someone a proficient reader. What skills did a "good" reader have that a "poor" reader lacked? After studying thousands of students identified as good readers, he produced a list of strategies used by these readers for both fiction and nonfiction texts.

Pearson's theory centres on the idea of metacognition, the ability to think about what we are reading. A good reader is aware of and is able to use and articulate the strategies that they use to interact with text and enhance meaning. Being a good reader goes beyond simply mastering the code of letter sounds. To be powerful readers, students must

- Make Connections: Strong readers relate what they are reading to personal experiences and background knowledge. This includes making text-to-self, text-to-text, and text-to-world connections.

- Visualize: Strong readers use the text to create a picture in their minds. This includes creating a multi-sensory image using sounds, sights, and smells.
- Ask Questions: Strong readers ask questions about the text as they are reading to enhance their comprehension. This includes asking literal and inferential questions before, during, and after reading.
- Make Inferences: Strong readers use evidence found in the text to fill in the blanks left by the author. They combine evidence from the text with their personal connections and background knowledge to make meaning.
- Analyze and Synthesize: Strong readers combine their thinking with the information from the text to draw conclusions and create new understandings. They are also able to take information from multiple sources and combine it for a specific purpose.
- Determine Importance: Strong readers sort through the information they read in the text and recognize the information that is important to their purpose for reading. They are able to distinguish between information that is interesting and information that enhances understanding.
- Monitor their Comprehension: Strong readers recognize when they are no longer understanding what they are reading and are able to go back and use different strategies to gain understanding.

Reading Strategies:

Making Connections
Asking Questions
Making Inferences
Analyzing/Synthesizing
Determining Importance
Monitoring Comprehension

As you can see, while fiction and nonfiction use some different strategies, they both incorporate connecting, questioning, inferring, and transforming.

Take a moment and examine the curriculum for your subject area. I think you would be hard pressed to not find words like *inferential*, *synthesize*, and *connections*.

In her first book, *Reading Power: Teaching Students to Think While They Read*, Adrienne Gear took Pearson's list and simplified it into five reading strategies for fiction. Good readers make connections, visualize, ask questions, make inferences, and transform their thinking based on what they read. In her second book, *Nonfiction Reading Power: Teaching students how to think while they read all kinds of information*, Adrienne introduced us to five reading strategies for reading nonfiction. Good readers of nonfiction make connections, zoom-in on text features, are able to determine importance, use questioning and inferring, and transform their thinking based on what they read.

All of these Reading Power strategies help readers monitor their comprehension because they bring the thinking that happens inside our heads into our consciousness. Once readers are aware of their thinking, they are better able to notice when their understanding goes off track.

Most secondary-school teachers can look at this list and recognize many of the skills we ask our students to master. However, when I first started teaching, I did little to actively teach my students these skills. The strategies uncovered by Pearson are not a natural progression that learners grow to understand once they are able to decode words. They are strategies that need to be explicitly taught to readers.

At the secondary level, students are often asked to go beyond the literal meaning of the texts that they read. As students move through the school system, the tasks they are assigned move away from the concrete toward the abstract. Students need more explicit instruction, not less, as the tasks and texts they are assigned become more complex.

We often ask older students to have discussions about what they read. The Reading Power strategies give students the language they need to talk about what they are reading. By modeling the language and giving students guidance in speaking and writing about their thoughts, we help them become both better readers and better communicators.

Metacognition

Simply put, metacognition involves being able to think about and communicate your thinking to others. Take a moment to consider this idea. Almost every waking moment of our lives involves thinking and making decisions based on this thinking. But this process happens inside of our minds, away from the eyes of anyone else. The thought process is hidden from view until we share our thoughts with others. By modeling our own thinking and providing students opportunities to practice sharing their thinking, we uncover the mystery surrounding what happens inside our heads.

I was speaking with a colleague from a neighboring district one day over lunch. We were discussing how engaged students are at the secondary level, observations prompted by a conversation she had had with her teenage son over the breakfast table that morning. He commented to her that he was lucky because "she had to go to school and think every day, but he got to go to school and check out." We looked at each other in horror at this statement, even though we both knew it to be true for most high-school students. The truth is that a focus on fact-based questions that have one correct answer rarely requires students to actually think about what they are learning. All they need to do is find the answer or, better yet, wait for someone else to find it and then memorize that answer. This *assign–assess* approach to comprehension is sadly evident in many high-school classrooms. Content-area teachers, in particular, do not feel that it is their job to teach comprehension skills: "They should already know how to read."

I knew this was evident in my own learning: I was always very successful in school because I was able to find the answer and memorize it. When I returned to school for graduate work in my 30s, it was a big adjustment for me. No one had ever asked me what I wanted to learn about or research. I was used to the teacher telling me what the assignment was, exactly how it should be done, and exactly what I needed to do to get an *A*. Thankfully, I found the professors that I worked with were great at modeling and providing practice experiences with inquiry and research.

Interacting with Text

Even as an avid reader, I never really thought about reading as being an interactive process. I thought everything I loved about books came from the text. I didn't think about what I, as the reader, brought to the reading party. After reading Pearson's research and Adrienne's explanation of the reading process, it all began to make sense. The reason some books appeal to some people and not to others is because we all bring something different to the reading experience.

Reader (experiences, memories, thoughts) + the text = comprehension

For many students, the reading equation shown here is a mystery. They mistakenly believe that all of the meaning is contained directly in the words written by the author. It is only through explicit instruction in reading strategies that this mystery can be uncovered for our students. Reading Power offers a structure for this explicit instruction.

Reading Power in the Classroom

Six Things I Believe to Be True About Literacy

1. Students need to read something meaningful, write something meaningful, and have an opportunity for meaningful conversations every day (Allington, 2002). The more we read and write, the better we become at it.
2. Students need the opportunity to choose the texts that they read. If we want students to read outside of the classroom, we need to provide opportunities for them to find and select texts that appeal to them.
3. Literacy cannot be taught only in the English or Language Arts classroom. Students need to be shown how these strategies apply to the things they read in other classes and in everyday life. All teachers are teachers of literacy.
4. Fiction and nonfiction are equally valuable. Typically, teachers of Language Arts focus on fiction in their classrooms, even though the majority of reading we do in our daily life is nonfiction. Students need direct instruction on how to read both types of text.
5. Good readers are not born that way. All students can become great readers with a little support. They need explicit instruction in reading comprehension strategies and multiple opportunities to practice these strategies.
6. While proficient readers might fully understand what they are reading, they may not be aware of how their brain makes sense of text. By teaching strategies like making thinking visible and tangible, and by providing students with a language to articulate their thinking, we can enhance both metacognitive awareness and comprehension in stronger readers.

Fiction Reading Power in Language Arts Classes

Those who teach in a linear system can adjust the timeline as needed. You may want to keep a similar structure, giving students a taste of all of the powers early in the year and then practicing with them as you interact with different texts throughout the rest of the school year.

Many high schools run on a semester system, so a teacher has a group of students for only five months. When teaching Senior English, I introduce Reading Power at the beginning of the year during my short-story unit. Plan to spend one to two weeks on each of the powers. This suggestion may send some teachers into a panic at the thought of that percentage of the semester being spent on the reading powers. But keep in mind I also cover the short-story unit during this time. Don't think of Reading Power as something new that you have to teach, but more as a layer you are adding to what you are already doing. As the semester progresses, make sure to incorporate each of the reading powers as you cover the other forms of literature, including the poetry, novels, and films or plays that your class interacts with. It is essential to continue to model all of the reading powers throughout the school year and to provide students time to practice these powers.

In my Language Arts class, I include a nonfiction unit near the beginning of the year, in which I explicitly teach the strategies specific to nonfiction. This allows me to incorporate a variety of nonfiction texts throughout the year to support the novels, plays, or poetry we are reading. Again, as with the fiction reading powers, it is essential to continue to model the powers and to create opportunities for students to continue to interact with the powers throughout the school year.

Some teachers prefer to teach using thematic units and to incorporate a variety of literary forms into a unit. If this is how you structure your classroom, you do not need to reorganize your whole program. You could focus on introducing the reading powers during your first unit or two, and then use the remaining units to practice the powers. You may need to add a few new texts to each unit to work as anchor texts for each reading power.

Sample Semester Plan: Secondary-School English Class

September	October	November	December	January
Short Story Unit	Short Story Unit	Literature Circles (Novels)	Literature Circles (Novels)	Poetry
Fiction Reading Powers • Connecting • Visualizing	Fiction Reading Powers • Questioning • Inferring • Transforming	Fiction Reading Powers • All	Fiction Reading Powers • All	Fiction Reading Powers • All
Nonfiction Reading Powers • Connecting • Zooming In	Nonfiction Reading Powers • Determining Importance • Questioning/Inferring • Transforming	Nonfiction Reading Powers • All	Nonfiction Reading Powers • All	Nonfiction Reading Powers • All

Nonfiction Reading Power in Content-Area Classes

In addition to Language Arts courses, I teach a variety of History and Social Studies courses. These courses provide me with a great platform to teach literacy skills to my students. Don't get me wrong—I teach History because I love it and I think the content is important for students to learn. However, the goal in these courses is not for students to memorize a bunch of facts. Rather, we want students to refine their research skills by improving their reading and writing skills. I truly believe that the content we teach is just a vehicle for helping our students become thinkers and learners. We explore the required content in my courses, but an equal amount of our time is spent practicing our reading, writing, and thinking. We explore the process of reading using texts related to the content we are learning about, including picture books and short stories, and we practice the reading powers using the nonfiction texts that I use to cover the content.

Plan to spend one to two weeks teaching each of the nonfiction reading powers. Once all of the powers have been introduced and practiced, continue to design learning activities that require students to apply what they have learned. For example, once we have learned how to determine importance, I continue to use the language and strategies with my students to practice that skill when note-taking and researching.

I have my students use a notebook as a Reading Journal in both my English and content-area classes. In English classes, students use the notebook to record their practice work for each of the powers and their response journals to various pieces of texts. In my content-area classes, students record their practice work, as well as any information they uncover about the topics we are studying. This allows me to see their growth as the year progresses and eliminates the problem of students searching through piles of loose papers.

When teaching history, sometimes I use fiction pieces when I can find texts that fit the content that we are studying. Good historical fiction is a great tool for teaching about events and time periods. I even use historical fiction as a writing task for students.

Sample Semester Plan: Content-Area Class

September	October	November	December	January
Nonfiction Reading Powers • Connecting • Zooming In	Nonfiction Reading Powers • Deter-mining Importance • Ques-tioning/ Inferring	Nonfiction Reading Powers • Trans-forming	Nonfiction Reading Powers • All	Nonfiction Reading Powers • All

Reading Power Beyond the Blocks

When I made the switch from teaching elementary school to teaching secondary school, I was amazed at how separate the blocks and classes were. In the beginning, I had no idea what students were learning in other subject areas unless I actually taught that course. I taught my English courses in total separation from my content-area courses. I rarely had conversations with my colleagues about what they were noticing about their students' literacy strengths and weaknesses. As the English teacher, the most I heard from my colleagues was complaints around what the students couldn't do when it came to reading and writing.

When I started writing this book, my goal was to bring all teachers into the literacy conversation. That is why I try to include ideas and lessons that would work in both Language Arts and content-area courses. If you are a Language Arts teacher, start a conversation with your content-area colleagues about ways to incorporate literacy instruction into their classes. If you are a content-area teacher, your Language Arts colleagues are a great resource for ideas to teach the literacy skills that students need to be successful in your area of study. It's time to start the conversation around literacy instruction in all classrooms.

This is my call for English and content-area teachers to unite! As an English teacher, talk to content-area colleagues who teach the same grades as you. Ask them about the subjects that they cover in their classes. Look for opportunities to incorporate fiction and nonfiction texts that support these topics. This could include using poetry, short stories, novels, or even picture books.

Ask content-area teachers which texts they use in their classes. These texts can offer you a source of nonfiction writing for your English classes. Explicit instruction on reading strategies for textbooks will help students in their content-area courses. It's a win–win situation!

In middle school, the amount of integration varies depending on the school. Some middle-school teachers work in specialty areas and may teach their subject areas to different classes of students throughout the day. Others have their students for all core academic subject areas (English, Social Studies, Math, Science); this makes integration between subject areas a lot easier.

Books listed are appropriate for use with high-school students. Those that could also be used in middle-school classes are marked with an M.

Sample Book List by Issue

ENVIRONMENT

Oryx and Crake; *The Year of the Flood* by Margaret Atwood (novels)
The Elephant Mountains by Scott Ely (novel, M)
The Lorax by Dr. Seuss (picture book, M)
Empty by Suzanne Weyn (novel, M)

ABORIGINAL STUDIES

Native Poetry in Canada: A Contemporary Anthology (poetry, M)
The Absolutely True Diary of a Part-Time Indian by Sherman Alexie (illustrated novel)

Peace Pipe Dreams: The Truth and Lies About Indians by Darrell Dennis (nonfiction)

When I Was Eight by Christy Gordon Fenton (picture book, M)

Secret of the Dance by Andrea Spalding (picture book, M)

A Man Called Raven by Richard van Camp (picture book, M)

THE MIDDLE AGES

Beowulf translated by Gareth Hinds (graphic novel)

DragonQuest by Allan Baillie (picture book, M)

In a Dark Wood; Raven of the Waves by Michael Cadnum (novels)

Macbeth by William Shakespeare (play)

"The Lady of Shalott" by Alfred Lord Tennyson (poem, M)

THE RENAISSANCE

Leonardo, the Beautiful Dreamer by Robert Byrd (picture book, M)

Ophelia by Lisa Klein (novel)

"The Highwayman" by Alfred Noyes (poem, M)

Starry Messenger: Galileo Galilei by Peter Sis (picture book, M)

Joan of Arc by Diane Stanley (picture book, M)

The Black Arrow by Robert Louis Stevenson (novel)

WORLD WAR I

A Corner of a Foreign Field: The Illustrated Poetry of the First World War (poetry anthology)

War Girls: A Collection of World War Stories Through the Eyes of Young Women by various authors (anthology, M)

Stay Where You Are and Then Leave by John Boyne (novel)

Shooting at the Stars: The Christmas Truce of 1914 by John Hendrix (picture book, M)

And the Soldiers Sang by J. Patrick Lewis (picture book, M)

Finding Winnie: The True Story of the World's Most Famous Bear by Lindsay Mattick (picture book, M)

Poems from the First World War by Gaby Morgan (poetry, M)

"Dulce et Decorum Est" by Wilfred Owen (poem)

"Attack" by Siegfried Sassoon (poem)

"An Irish Airman Foresees His Death" by William Butler Yeats (poem)

WORLD WAR II

Code Talkers by Joseph Bruchac (novel)

Terrible Things: An Allegory of the Holocaust by Eve Bunting (picture book, M)

Rose Blanche by Christophe Gallaz (picture book, M)

The Harmonica by Tony Johnston (picture book, M)

The Hidden Girl: A True Story of the Holocaust by Lola Rein Kaufman (novel, M)

"What Do I Remember of the Evacuation" by Joy Kogawa (poem)

Number the Stars (novel, M); *Crow Call* (picture book, M) by Lois Lowry

Barbed Wire Baseball: How One Man Brought Hope to the Japanese Internment Camps by Marissa Moss (picture book, M)

Erika's Story by Ruth Vander Zee (picture book, M)

Surviving Hitler: A Boy in the Nazi Death Camps by Andrea Warren (nonfiction, M)

Code Name Verity by Elizabeth Wein (novel)

The Book Thief by Markus Zusak (novel)

Lesson Using Content-Area Texts

- Ask students to bring a textbook from their Social Studies or Science class. It can be a good idea to borrow a few textbooks from your colleagues for the students who forget to bring one. Students can also work in pairs with one textbook if not everyone has a book.
- Put your list of nonfiction text features in a prominent place in your classroom and direct students' attention to it.

See page 92 for the Text Features chart.

- Tell students that they are going on a treasure hunt to find examples of the text features in their textbooks. When they find one, they will record it on their Text Features chart (page 92), including the page number, a quote or sketch of the example, and a description of the information that is communicated by the example.
- Collect filled-in charts from students for formative assessment.

Information Sharing

See page 21 for more on nonfiction reading assessment.

Share your reading assessment results with other teachers who teach your students. Better yet, work with content-area teachers to conduct a nonfiction reading assessment in their classrooms. After all, there is no point in conducting multiple reading assessments on the same students in their different courses. Look for trends in student weaknesses and work collaboratively as a school to look for ways to address these weaknesses in all classes.

Research Projects

Look for writing opportunities from students' work in content-area classes. Consider working with your students' other teachers to design authentic writing activities that students can work on in both classes. Students can use their content-area class time for research and information gathering, and their Language Arts time to refine their writing skills.

Cross-curricular collaborative inquiry projects are a great fit for many current curricula; e.g., the redesigned curriculum in British Columbia.

For example, your school could set up a research week, during which students focus on inquiry-based research projects based on their content-area classes or areas of interest. English teachers can be paired with content-area teachers to work with students on the writing process, with the content-area teachers supporting the research component. Assessment is a team effort, with English teachers marking the writing and content-area teachers marking the content. These research projects could be used as part of a learning celebration with parents and community members.

Vocabulary

All teachers need to focus on increasing students' vocabulary and on providing students with strategies to use when they encounter unfamiliar words. What if all the teachers in a school got together and developed a list of prefixes, suffixes, and root words that students need to know at each grade in order to understand the subject-area vocabulary? For example, in Math, students may need to know the number prefixes (*mono-*, *di-*, *tri-*, *tetra-*, etc) for their geometry units. For Science, students may need to know root words common to biology (*derm*, *hemo*, *cardi*, *cerebr*). Social Studies might require understanding of concept words (*immigration*, *emigration*, *demography*).

There are several strategies both English and content-area teachers can share for developing key vocabulary.

ANCHOR CHARTS OR VOCABULARY WALLS

Work as a class to design charts or word walls exploring the meaning of important vocabulary words. They might include definitions, illustrations, and/or connections between the various terms.

WORD MAPS

Work with students to develop word maps for key vocabulary words they need to know for their content-area classes. The goal behind word maps is to build connections between the word and students' background knowledge to create meaning. The are many different ways to make word maps, and many different connections to focus on, depending on the word. For example, you could map *meaning*, *example*, *non-example*, and *illustration*. Another example would be to map *meaning*, *root word*, *similar words that use the same root*, and *connection to topic of study*.

Concept	Definition
Covalent Bond	*A chemical bond where atoms share electrons*
Example	Non-example
CO$_2$	*ionic bond where atoms transfer electrons* *NaCl*

MODEL YOUR THINKING

As you read through texts, explain how you are able to figure out the meaning of unfamiliar words using your knowledge of root words. Even if you know the meaning of the word, pretend that you don't and use it as a teaching opportunity. For example, when reading a chemistry text, you might approach it this way:

"Covalent bonds." Huh, I don't know what that means. I know that "co" means together, and "val" means strength. So I'm going to make an educated guess that it means something about strong together. Can someone look up the meaning for me?

Once someone has located the meaning, discuss how close you were:

Okay, so "covalent" means it's a chemical bond where atoms share electrons. I think I was on the right track with my initial thought, but now I can readjust my thinking with this new knowledge.

These modeling conversations help students see the worth of knowing root words and the importance of not simply reading on when you don't understand something.

2 Introducing Reading Power to Students

Introducing the Reading Powers

In this lesson, students are introduced to the strategies, or reading powers, that good readers use when trying to comprehend text.

In this lesson, the teacher will facilitate a conversation around what it means to be a good reader.

- Start the lesson by asking students to think way back to when they were children learning to read. Ask them if they remember some of the things they had to learn in order to read. They will probably come up with things like the alphabet song, which sound went with each letter, reading from left to right, and sounding out words. Most of the suggestions will probably have to do with decoding words as opposed to understanding what the words mean.
- Make a list of student answers on the board. Explain to students that these skills are only one part of reading.
- Ask students what things they have learned about reading in the last few years. Students usually have a harder time answering this question. They will probably talk about activities like *answering questions about reading* or *writing paragraphs or essays about what they have read*. Prompt students to think about how they were taught to understand what they read.
- Record their answers in a chart showing the difference between decoding and thinking.

SKILLS OF PROFICIENT READERS

Decoding	Thinking
phonetic awareness (letters and sounds)	comprehension
spelling	understanding
punctuation	constructing meaning
fluency	metacognition

- Ask students about what it means to be a good reader. See if they can come up with some of the thinking strategies that good readers use. If your students have learned the reading powers in previous grades, they should be able to come up with a list of strategies. If they haven't been introduced to Reading Power, you will need to lead them to the metacognitive strategies of connecting, visualizing, questioning, inferring, synthesizing, determining importance, and monitoring comprehension.
- Finally, talk with students about Pearson's research and what it tells us about how to be a good reader. Explain that there are two skill sets that need to be activated when someone is reading: decoding the words in the book is one, and thinking about what those words mean is the other. The problem is that the words on the page are concrete (you can see them) but thinking is abstract

(we can't see it or hold it). So when someone tells you to "think" when you read, what does that look like? "Thinking" is connecting, visualizing, questioning, inferring, and transforming. Tell students that over the next few weeks, the class will be learning about and practicing with each of the reading powers to become more powerful readers.

Knowing What Your Students Know

"I don't know how you can teach kids until you know what they know." (Boushey and Moser, 2009)

After the initial introduction to the Reading Power strategies, do a reading assessment, focusing on the thinking skills that students have, rather than on diagnosing a specific reading level. There are other assessments out there that will provide you with a number or grade-level score. Your school probably has access to a variety of these tests. From this assessment, however, you want to know what strategies students are able to use and which ones they have trouble with.

I begin each of my courses, whether Language Arts–based or content area, with a quick reading assessment.

I strongly encourage you to collaborate with your colleagues whenever possible to administer and mark these assessments. After all, this is good information that all teachers should have about their students. Perhaps the fiction assessment can be done by the English teacher and the nonfiction assessment by the Social Studies or Science teacher, so that all students in each grade level complete both assessments. If you do both assessments in your classroom, try to spread them out over a few days or weeks. The students won't want to do assessments one right after the other, and you won't want to mark two assessments at the same time either.

Fiction Reading Assessment

See page 23 for the Fiction Reading Assessment; page 25 for the Fiction Reading Rubric.

- Review the reading powers you discussed in the introductory lesson (page 19).
- Tell students that you want to know what their strengths and struggles are as readers. Assure them that this assessment won't affect their grade in your course. Tell them that you want to know what reading strategies they need to practice and what strategies they are already good at. It might help to explain that you don't want to bore them by teaching them things that they already know how to do.
- Hand out the reading assessment on pages 23–24. Go over each of the questions and provide examples of each strategy.
- Hand out copies of the text.

See page 22 for more on choosing texts.

- Give students time to read the story independently and answer the questions. If students finish early, encourage them to add more detail to their responses.
- Collect and assess, using the Fiction Reading Rubric on page 25.
- Look for areas where your class struggles. This assessment should tell you which powers you need to spend more time on, and which powers you can move through more quickly.

"Written output is rarely a reflection of cognitive ability. Remember that you are assessing your students' ability to think and not their ability to write." (Gear, 2015)

If I know I have students who are not reading at grade level, I may provide them with a different text to read, or have someone read the text to them so they can focus on the strategies rather than struggle with decoding. Students who struggle with written output can communicate their responses verbally and be assessed based on what they can tell you about the text.

Nonfiction Reading Assessment

See page 26 for the Nonfiction Reading Assessment; page 28 for the Nonfiction Reading Rubric.

- Review the Reading Power strategies from the introductory lesson on page 19.
- Tell students that you want to assess their strengths and struggles as readers. Assure them that this assessment won't affect their grade in the course. Tell them that you want to know what reading skills they need to practice and what skills that they are already good at. It might help to explain that you don't want to spend time teaching them things that they already know how to do.
- Hand out the reading assessment on pages 26–27. Go over each of the questions and provide examples of each strategy.
- Hand out copies of the text.

See page 22 for more on choosing texts.

- Give students time to read the text independently and answer the questions. If students finish early, encourage them to add more detail to their responses.
- Collect and assess, using the Nonfiction Reading Rubric on page 28.
- Look for areas where your class struggles. This assessment should tell you which powers you may need to spend more time on, and which powers you can move through more quickly.

Teaching Reading Power

As I have mentioned, when I first started teaching secondary school, I did a lot more assigning and assessing than I did teaching. In my content-area classes, I would explicitly teach the content, but I expected my students to have the reading skills to access the information and the writing skills to communicate their understanding. I mistakenly thought that the more my students read and wrote, the better they would get. I relied on implicit instruction to teach the literacy skills that I wanted my students to develop.

This lack of explicit instruction carried over into my English classes. I wrongly assumed that my students already knew all there was to know about reading, and that all I had to do was assign reading tasks. I was more focused on getting students to do things than on teaching them literacy skills; I mistakenly believed that these were the same things.

"Teacher consistently provides direct, explicit modelling of **cognitive strategies** used by readers to engage in text." (Richard Allington, 2002, on the Six T's of Effective Literary Instruction)

Reading Power follows a *gradual release of responsibility* model. Students first need to see someone modeling the skill that they are trying to learn. This part is essential to the process because it allows students to see the skill rather than just learn about it. Next, students need time to practice with their peers and receive feedback. This stage allows students who are ready to explore the skill to do so, while those who aren't there yet can see the skill modeled by others. During the third stage, students practice independently while still receiving feedback from the teacher. It is only after students have had sufficient practice with the skill that they move on to its application.

- Direct Instruction and Modeling: This is the explicit teaching part of the process. The teacher introduces the power, and models and shares his/her thinking. While this can be a bit uncomfortable in the beginning and can feel unnatural, it is essential that you make your thinking visible for your students.
- Guided Practice: Students practice and share their learning with their classmates while getting feedback from the teacher. In working with their peers, students who require more support will have multiple opportunities to see the skill in action.

- Independent Practice: Students practice using the powers in structured tasks while getting guidance and feedback from the teacher. This stage allows students to refine their individual skills.
- Application: Students use the powers independently while engaging with a variety of texts. This is the only stage that should be used for summative assessment.

How Much Time Should I Spend on Each Power?

The answer to this question is really quite simple: It depends on your students. You may find that some students have had a really strong introduction to some or all of the reading powers in previous classes. You may find that some students have never been explicitly taught strategies for thinking about what they are reading. These students will likely need a lot more modeling and practice time when learning the strategies. You will have to judge where your students are based on your reading assessment (see pages 23–24, 26–27) and your conversations with students during the introductory lesson (see page 19). Most of the lessons in this book include a product that you can collect for formative assessment, to inform you if your students need more practice on a certain concept.

How Do I Choose Texts?

"If we continue to teach students new comprehension strategies with texts that are at the *edge of their competence,* we risk the danger of burdening their learning rather than enhancing it. " — Richard Allington, Provincial Reading Conference Keynote, Vancouver, 2009

I like to introduce the reading powers to students using a text that is below current grade level. Sometimes I use picture books; sometimes I use a short story or a short excerpt from a different form of text. I read the first story or text to students out loud so that they can focus on their thinking rather than on decoding. This also provides a level entry point for students who are not reading at grade level. My focus in the beginning lessons is to allow students an opportunity to think about the text and to practice the reading strategy rather than practice decoding the words.

You can differentiate your lessons through the texts that you use with your students. For each fiction power, I have included a list of short stories, novels, picture books, and plays. For the nonfiction powers, I have not included a list for each power, but rather some suggestions for places to access quality nonfiction pieces. When students are working on independent practice, you can provide a variety of texts at different reading levels for them to use. That way, even if they are not reading at grade level, they can still be practicing the skills you are focusing on.

"Just as many have recommended using texts in decoding instruction that emphasize the particular sound–letter relationship that students are learning, we recommend linking closely the comprehension strategy being taught to the texts to which it is initially applied and practiced." (Duke & Pearson, 2002)

The bottom line is that you are the best judge of which texts will work for your students. You know their abilities and their interests. You know which texts you have access to in your school. You probably also have books and resources that hold a special place in your heart. That's the great thing about teaching these reading strategies. You don't have to abandon your go-to favorites and purchase a bunch of new resources. You just need to look at your resources through a different lens to see what powers they best support. In my experience, now that the Reading Power strategies are in my consciousness, it is very obvious when I read new texts—or old favorites—how they support the powers.

Fiction Reading Assessment

Name: _____	Date: _____

Summarize: What is this text about?

Connecting: What connections can you make between the text and your own life, between the text and other stories you have read or seen, or between the text and things that are happening in the world? How do these connections help you better understand the text?

Visualizing: Sketch some of the images that came to mind while you were reading the text. What did you see, hear, or feel while reading?

Pembroke Publishers © 2016 *Powerful Readers* by Kyla Hadden and Adrienne Gear ISBN 978-1-55138-313-2

Fiction Reading Assessment (continued)

Questioning: What are some questions that you have before, during, and after reading the text?

Inferring: What are some things that you believe to be true, but the author didn't come right out and say in the text? What part of the text made you think this?

Transforming: What can the reader learn about life from this story? What message was the author trying to communicate through the text? What are you thinking about now that you weren't thinking about before you read the text?

Pembroke Publishers © 2016 *Powerful Readers* by Kyla Hadden and Adrienne Gear ISBN 978-1-55138-313-2

Fiction Reading Rubric

	Not Meeting	Minimally Meeting	Fully Meeting	Exceeding
Connecting	Is unable to make any connections to the text.	Finds one or two surface-level connections to the text; most connections are text-to-self connections.	Finds multiple personal and meaningful connections to the text; is able to connect to self, other texts, and the world.	Finds meaningful connections to the text and is able to explain how the connections help understanding.
Visualizing	Is unable to describe any visual images from the text.	Is able to describe some visual images from the text; images are not always connected to meaningful parts of the text.	Is able to describe visual images from the text that are connected to meaningful parts of the text.	Is able to describe visual images using multiple senses that are connected to meaningful parts of the text; can explain how this helps understanding.
Questioning	Is unable to generate any questions about the text.	Generates one or two quick-thinking (literal) questions about the text.	Generates a mixture of quick- and deep-thinking questions about the text.	Generates multiple deep-thinking questions about the text.
Inferring	Is unable to identify any information that is not directly written in the text.	Is able to communicate simple inferences but has difficulty supporting them with evidence from the text; sometimes inferences do not enhance the meaning of the story.	Is able to communicate meaningful inferences; can support them with evidence from the text; can provide some explanations for them.	Is able to communicate meaningful inferences and can support them with highly relevant references from the text and personal experiences; can explain how these inferences have enhanced understanding.
Transforming	Is unable to identify any important issues in the text.	Can identify the main message or theme from the text but is unable to explain how the message might affect the reader.	Can identify the main message or theme from the text and is able to explain how the message might affect the reader.	Can identify the main message from the text and is able to explain how the message might affect his or her own life.

Pembroke Publishers © 2016 *Powerful Readers* by Kyla Hadden and Adrienne Gear ISBN 978-1-55138-313-2

Nonfiction Reading Assessment

Name:	Date:

Connecting: How does what you read connect with what you already knew? Explain your connection(s).

Text Features: What are some of the different text features used in this text? What kind of information do they communicate? Why did the author choose these text features?

Summarizing: What are the main ideas from this text?

Pembroke Publishers © 2016 *Powerful Readers* by Kyla Hadden and Adrienne Gear ISBN 978-1-55138-313-2

Nonfiction Reading Assessment (continued)

Questioning: What are some questions that you have before, during, and after reading this text?

Inferring: What is something not written in the text or shown in the visuals that you are now thinking about?

Transforming: What are you thinking about now that you might not have considered before? How did the information in this text change your understanding? Explain.

Nonfiction Reading Rubric

	Not Meeting	Minimally Meeting	Fully Meeting	Exceeding
Connecting	Is unable to make any connections to the text.	Makes one or two "quick" surface-level connections to the text.	Uses background knowledge and experiences to make relevant connections to the text.	Makes meaningful connections to the text and is able to communicate how these connections enhance understanding.
Zooming In (Text Features)	Is unable to identify any text features in the text.	Can identify some text features by name.	Can identify multiple text features by name; can describe how they are used and the information they include.	Can identify multiple text features by name and is able to extract and explain the information located in the text features; understands how writers use text features to organize information.
Determining Importance (Summarizing)	Is unable to identify any important information or big ideas from the text.	Identifies the main idea from the text and is able to identify some details.	Identifies the main idea from the text and is able to identify most of the important supporting details.	Identifies the main idea from the text and is able to identify important supporting details; demonstrates understanding of text structure.
Questioning/ Inferring	Is unable to generate any questions about the text; cannot communicate any information that is not directly written in the text.	Generates one or two quick-thinking questions about the text; is able to make some simple inferences that might not be important to the meaning of the text.	Generates a mixture of quick- and deep-thinking questions about the text; is able to make meaningful inferences.	Generates multiple deep-thinking questions about the text; uses inferences to generate answers to questions to enhance understanding.
Transforming	Is unable to identify any change in thinking from the text.	Is able to identify some new facts from the text.	Is able to identify new thinking based on the text.	Is able to communicate how the new information in the text fits in with his/her initial thinking.

Pembroke Publishers © 2016 *Powerful Readers* by Kyla Hadden and Adrienne Gear ISBN 978-1-55138-313-2

Fiction Reading Power

Once students have mastered the decoding part of reading, they still need to be thinking while they read. Reading comprehension requires an active interaction between the reader and the text. There has been a lot of research, by Pearson and others, on what this thinking while reading looks like. These are the five strategies that are most relevant to reading fiction.

CONNECTING

Powerful readers are able to make connections between the text and their own experiences and knowledge. While connecting is often the easiest reading power for students to grasp, it is also the most important because it forms the foundation for all the other strategies. Readers must access their own schema in order to visualize, question, infer, and transform their thinking.

VISUALIZING

Powerful readers are able to use their background knowledge to form mental images in their heads. Visualizing enhances the reader's understanding by providing concrete images of the abstract ideas presented in the text. Even though the image is only in the reader's head, it is created by something concrete that the reader has seen or experienced.

QUESTIONING

Powerful readers are able to generate questions while they read. These questions can be clarifying questions focused on correcting misunderstandings, predicting questions focused on events in the story, or deep-thinking questions that take the reader beyond the literal text. The important part is that students are thinking and asking questions while they read.

INFERRING

Powerful readers are able to use their background knowledge to think beyond the text and add information. They are able to connect the author's words with their own experiences to fill in the parts that are not explicitly written. Readers who can infer understand that many authors leave some things for the reader to figure out on their own.

TRANSFORMING

Powerful readers understand that stories have the ability to change the way we think about ourselves, others, and the world. While some stories are simply for entertainment, many stories allow readers to explore what it means to be human. Transforming requires the reader to use all the Reading Power strategies to uncover personal meaning from stories.

3 Connecting

In her revised edition of *Reading Power*, Adrienne Gear refers to "brain pockets" as the source for our connections. She explains to students that thinking is organized and stored into three areas or "pockets" of our brain: experiences are stored in the Memory Pocket, information is stored in the Fact Pocket, and creative thinking is stored in the Imagination Pocket. Depending on what type of text we are reading, we go to different pockets to find our connections. Making thinking visible in this way can help make connections more accessible.

Connecting allows readers to better understand the text based on their memories, experiences, and knowledge. Sometimes when we read things, we feel an emotional response to certain characters and events because we have experienced something similar, read or viewed something similar, or have learned about something similar. If we have a shared experience, we can form a text-to-self connection. If we have read or viewed something similar, we can form a text-to-text connection. If we have learned about something similar, we can make a text-to-world connection. The more meaningful the connection, the stronger the reader's response is to the text.

Connecting may seem like the simplest of all of the reading powers, but it is an essential part of many of the other powers. Students who cannot make connections to what they read will not be able to visualize or make inferences. In addition, students who cannot make text-to-text connections are unable to do compare-and-contrast activities involving pieces of literature. While there really isn't an order for teaching the reading powers, I would argue that connecting forms the foundation for all the other powers. For example, it is almost impossible to make inferences about how a character is feeling if you have no experience or understanding of what they are going through. Even if we haven't experienced something similar (text–self), we can base our response on something we have read or viewed (text–text) or on something that is happening in the world (text–world).

I like to introduce students to the idea of connecting by asking them to think of people in their lives they feel a connection to. We talk about how different things connect us to different people: we might share similar ideas and values with some people; we might connect to other people who have interests similar to our own. Usually, our closest connections are to the people we have shared experiences with. Ask students to recount their emotions during some common life experiences, such as the first day of high school or how they feel before a big test. Most of us probably feel similar emotions during these events. This allows us to feel connected to others when they experience similar events.

I then lead students into a discussion around characters from books or movies that they connect to. It's easy to get students talking about their favorites. Most of us have had the experience of being emotional when something bad happens to a character. Many of us have openly cried when reading a book or watching a movie. I ask students why we feel emotions when we read or watch other people's stories. Usually, it's because we connect to what is happening to that character. Empathy is connecting at its finest! Emotional connections are likely the strongest and most powerful connections we can make and are often referred to as "deep-thinking" connections. Most students will be able to identify something they connect to even if they didn't realize that they were connecting.

Sequential Lessons for Connecting

Lesson 1 (Teacher-Directed): Introducing the Power

This lesson focuses on introducing the different types of connections that readers can make.

For this lesson, the teacher will model his or her connections; students will sort the connections as text-to-self, text-to-text, and text-to-world.

- Introduce the Reading Power of Connecting by telling students that powerful readers use their background knowledge to help them make meaning of texts. Our experiences help us understand characters, their motivations, and their feelings.
- Discuss the idea that we can make connections to our own experiences (text-to-self), to things we have read or viewed (text-to-text), or to things that are happening in the world (text-to-world).
- Select a short text to read to students. Make sure it is something that you, yourself, can make a lot of connections to, as you will be modeling the power for students.
- Tell students that while you read, they need to record the connections you are modeling on a piece of paper, leaving space in between each connection. I like to start by having students examine my connections, so that they have a sample of quality connections to work with.

I like to use a picture book that can be read from start to finish in one lesson. My go-to book for modeling connecting is *Twelve Terrible Things* by Marty Kelley, because there are a number of pictures in the story that really remind me of my childhood.

- Read the story to students, pausing a few times during reading to share your connections. When you are finished reading the story, give students a few moments to finish recording your connections.
- Ask students what your first connection was. Once they have identified the connection, tell them how this connection helped you understand the text. Have students record your thinking on the same sheet where they recorded your original connections.
- Finally, have students reflect on what they noticed and learned about making connections. Students can either talk to a partner or write a short reflection on the bottom of their sheet. Collect sheets for formative assessment.

Lesson 2 (Guided Practice): Interacting with the Power

This lesson focuses on the unique nature of connections.

For this lesson, students will practice making connections and explore how connections develop from the reader's experiences.

- Review the Reading Power of Connecting and discuss the idea of text–self, text–text, and text–world connections. Remind students that connecting helps the reader better understand characters, their motivations, and their feelings.
- Pass out sticky notes and explain that students will be recording their own connections to a story you will be reading to them. Ask students not to put their names on the sticky notes, as they will be used again in the next lesson.

Texts that I recommend for this lesson include *Bully* by Patricia Polacco and *Saturday Climbing* by W.D. Valgardson.

- Select a story to read to students that has a lot of places where teenagers can make connections. I prefer to read the story aloud so that students are not struggling with the decoding part of reading. When you read the story to students, they all can practice making connections, regardless of their independent reading level.
- Introduce the story to students and provide some background information. This could include information about the author, the context, or the plot of the story. Once you have introduced the story, ask students if anyone is already making connections to the story. If they are, remind them to write their connections on their sticky notes.

- Begin reading the story, pausing partway through the reading to give students time to record their connections. It is important that you continue to model your thinking so be sure to share out any connections that you are making to the story. When you finish reading, give students a few moments to write down any remaining connections.
- Provide an opportunity for students to share out their connections. As students are sharing, discuss the fact that, even though you were all hearing the same story, the connections each person came up with are unique. This is due to the fact that everyone has different perspectives, experiences, and memories that provide them with different points of connection. Explain that is one of the reasons why certain people feel strong connections to some texts while others don't.
- If time allows, try grouping or sorting the connections. See if you can create a sticky-note graph of similar connections.
- End the lesson by asking students to share (or write) what they learned or noticed about making connections. Collect the sticky notes for use in the next lesson.

Lesson 3 (Guided Practice): Interacting with the Power

In this lesson, students will sort connections from the previous lesson as text-to-self, text-to-text, or text-to-world. They will then add information about how different connections enhance comprehension.

This lesson focuses on identifying the different kinds of connections and how they enhance the reader's understanding.

- Put the three categories of connections on the board or a projected screen (text–self, text–text, text–world). Hand each student one of the student connection sticky notes from Lesson 2 (page 31). Have each student bring a connection up to the front and place it in the correct category. Discuss as a group and make sure they are all in the correct place.
- Introduce students to the idea of basic (quick) connections and quality (deep-thinking) connections. In order for something to move into the category of a quality connection, it needs to help them understand something about the book. For example, "I have a pair of black shoes just like the main character" probably doesn't teach you anything about the story. Something like "I have played in a championship soccer game so I understand that the main character probably felt a little nervous and really excited" enhances the reader's understanding of the story.
- Write two new categories on the board, *Basic* and *Quality*. You can use *Quick* and *Deep-Thinking* if that is what your students are used to. Using the sticky notes that are already on the board, work as a group to divide the connections between the two categories. As you look at each connection, brainstorm how each connection could enhance the reader's understanding of the story.
- Have students select three connections from the board (they can choose their own or someone else's). Students record each connection, identify it as a text–self, text–text, or text–world connection, and explain how it helped the reader's understanding of the story. They might want to use the Looking at Connections chart on page 37.
- At this point, it can be helpful to give students sentence starters to help them communicate their connections. See samples on page 33. Collect the responses for formative assessment.

See page 37 for the Looking at Connections chart.

Sample Sentence Starters

Text–Self

- What I just read reminds me of _____. This helps me understand the text because _____.
- I understand _____ because in my own experience _____.

Text–Text

- The _____ in this text is similar to when _____ in (book, movie, story). This makes me think that _____.
- I understand _____ because in _____ (book, movie, story) _____ (explain what happened).

Text–World

- What I read makes me think of _____ (current or past event) because _____.
- I understand _____ because I know about _____ (current or past event).

Lesson 4 (Guided Practice): Interacting with the Power

This lesson focuses on linking connections to events in the text.

In this lesson, students will practice making connections and connecting them back to events in the text.

- Select a grade-level text with multiple points for teenagers to connect to. The story also needs to have a traditional plot structure, with rising action, climax, and falling action.
- Provide students with sticky notes for recording their connections. Tell them that while you read, they need to record on the sticky notes their connections and the part in the story that made them have the connection (this part will play a key role in the next part of the lesson).
- Read the story to students, pausing to give them time to record their connections. When you finish reading, give students a few moments to write down any remaining connections.
- With students' help, create a large plot diagram on a bulletin board; the board needs to be big enough so that posters students will create later in the lesson will fit around it. Work as a class to select the main events for the rising action, the climax, and important events during the falling action.
- Have students select their best connection and put that sticky note on the class plot diagram next to the point in the story that made them have the connection. They may need to look back in the story to see where their connection happened in relation to the main events.
- Have students create a one-page poster containing a picture or symbol for their connection and a short paragraph linking their connection to the text, explaining how it enhanced their understanding of the text. It can be helpful

to provide students with paragraph outlines and sentence starters to connect their connections to the text; see examples below.

- Finally, have students staple their connection posters to the bulletin board. Using string, students connect their posters to the points in the story that made them have their connections. This will provide students with a visual, not only of their own connection, but also of the connections made by their peers, and how these connections are connected to events in the story.
- End the lesson by asking the students to share or record what they learned and noticed about connecting to events. Posters can be used as formative assessment.

Sample Sentence Starters

- My connection to the story is _____.
  When _____ happened, it made me think of
  _____ because _____.
  This helped me understand that _____.
- In the story I thought about _____ when
  _____. This makes me think that _____
  _____ because _____.

Lesson 5 (Guided Practice): Interacting with the Power

In this lesson, students think back to memorable texts that they have encountered in their lives.

- Remind students of the three different kinds of connections (text-to-self, text-to-text, and text-to-world).
- Ask students to think back to stories and novels that they have read in the past (or movies or TV shows if they can't think of any stories or books). It could be a childhood favorite from years ago or a novel that they read last week. It might be helpful to share out and make a list on the board of class favorites to help jog the memory of students who can't think of a favorite story. It would also be a good time to share some of your favorites with students.
- Ask students to think back to why they like these particular texts. Remind them of the idea of quality connections. We may enjoy some titles because they are funny and they entertain us, but we are looking for deep connections that help us better understand the text. Again, it would be helpful to share one or two of your connections to your favorite texts.
- Once some students have had a chance to share their connections to their favorite texts, ask them to take out a piece of paper and jot down their thoughts and connections to their text. They can comment on what they love about the book and why they still remember it, but they have to include a personal connection to it. They also need to be able to link their connections to particular events in the text, and to explain how it enhanced their understanding or made an impact on them.
- When everyone has a rough list of their thoughts and connections, have students write a paragraph about their favorite text. It may be helpful to provide students with a paragraph outline or sentence starters before they begin (see Lesson 4 on page 33).
- Collect student writing for formative assessment.

The focus of this lesson is practicing making connections to events in texts that have been read and explaining how the connections enhanced understanding of the text.

I like to bring a copy of one of the Baby-sitters Club books. These were my go-to novels during middle school because I connected to the feelings experienced by the female main characters.

The focus of this lesson is demonstrating the ability to use connections to enhance comprehension.

Lesson 6 (Independent Practice): Using the Power

In this lesson, students apply what they have learned about connections in a written paragraph.

- Select a grade-level story that provides multiple places for teenagers to connect.
- You could give students sticky notes to use if they want to jot down their connections as they are reading. If they have a photocopy of the story, they can write their connections right on the copy.
- Have students write a paragraph about their top three connections. For each connection, they need to describe the connection, identify the part of the story that made them think of the connection, and state what the connection taught them about the story.
- Collect student writing for summative assessment.

ASSESSMENT RUBRIC FOR CONNECTING

Key
NYM = Not Yet Meeting
M = Meeting
FM = Fully Meeting
EX = Exceeding

Making Connections	NYM	M	FM	EX
Is able to make connections to background knowledge and experiences				
Recognizes the difference between text-to-self, text-to-text, and text-to-world connections				
Is able to make connections between multiple texts				
Can explain how a connection extends thinking				

Focus Literary Device: Point of View

In middle school, students should understand the difference between first-person and third-person narration. In secondary school, students should be able to differentiate between the three types of third-person narration.

At some point during lessons on connecting, I like to bring up the idea of point of view. By secondary school, students are expected to be able to distinguish between first-person narration and objective, limited-omniscient, and omniscient points of view. I used to find that, at best, students were able to regurgitate the definition of these terms, and were sometimes able to identify which one was used in the narration of a story. While students need to be able to identify the various points of view in texts, it is more important that they understand how the author's choice of narration affects the meaning of the story.

At the beginning of my short-story unit, I introduce students to the different types of narration. I usually supply excerpts from different texts as examples of the three types. I then have a discussion about which type of narration is easier to connect to. It is sometimes more difficult to connect to objective stories because we have to infer all of the characters' feelings. Usually, omniscient is the easiest to connect to because we have a greater understanding of multiple characters to base those connections on.

Sample Lesson: Whose Story Is Missing?

This lesson works best with complex stories with multiple characters.

- Read a short story to students or have them read the story independently.
- Have students create a plot diagram for the story.

This lesson also encourages inferring.

- Beside each event, have students write a few sentences describing how one character would have described or felt about each event.
- Then have students select another character and write a few sentences about how that character would have described or felt about each event.

Prompts and Sentence Frames to Encourage Connecting

- Describe something you have read or watched that is similar to something in this text.
- Describe something you have experienced that is similar to something in this text.
- Describe the similarities between you and one of the main characters.
- Pick an experience from your own life and describe how it helped you understand the text.
- Select a quote from the text that you connect to and describe your connection.
- *This text connects to my life because…*
- What character is most like you? Describe how he or she is similar to you.
- Describe a time when you faced a similar situation to one experienced by a character in the text.
- Describe a time that you felt the same way as one of the characters in the text. What was happening to cause you to feel that way?
- Describe a situation that is happening in the world that is similar to something that happened in the text.

Books listed are appropriate for use with high-school students. Those that could also be used in middle-school classes are marked with an M.

Suggested Texts for Connecting

Winter Girls by Laurie Halse Anderson (novel)
"Still I Rise" by Maya Angelou (poem)
"Refugee Blues" by W.H. Auden (poem, M)
"The Truth About Sharks" by Joan Bauer (short story, M)
"Gentlemen, Your Verdict" by Michael Bruce (short story, M)
The Perks of Being a Wallflower by Stephen Chbosky (novel)
"The One Who Watches" by Judith Ortiz Cofer (short story, M)
"Another Reason Why I Don't Keep a Gun in the House" by Billy Collins (poem)
"Catch" by Sarah Ellis (short story, M)
If I Stay by Gayle Forman (novel)
"The Badness Within Him" by Susan Hill (short story, M)
The Outsiders by S.E. Hinton (novel, M)
Confessions of a Former Bully by Trudy Ludwig (picture book, M)

Too Perfect by Trudy Ludwig (picture book, M)
"Button, Button" by Richard Matheson (short story)
"TLA" by Jane McFann (short story)
Crazy by Han Nolan (novel, M)
"Barbie Doll" by Marge Piercy (poem)
Bully by Patricia Polacco (picture book, M)
"Words" by Dian Curtis Regan (short story, M)
A Midsummer Night's Dream by William Shakespeare (play, M)
Romeo and Juliet by William Shakespeare (play, M)
Star Girl by Jerry Spinelli (novel, M)
Deadly Loyalties by Jennifer Storm (novel, strong content)
"Saturday Climbing" by W.D. Valgardson (short story)
Flipped by Wendelin Van Draanen (novel, M)
"Someone Who Used to Have Someone" by Miriam Waddington (poem)
Empty by Suzanne Weyn (novel, M)

Looking at Connections

Connection	Text–Self	Text–Text	Text–World	How this connection enhances my understanding

4   Visualizing

"I love books, by the way, way more than movies. Movies tell you what to think. A good book lets you choose a few thoughts for yourself. Movies show you the pink house. A good book tells you there's a pink house and lets you paint some of the finishing touches, maybe choose the roof style, park your own car out front. My imagination has always topped anything a movie could come up with." — Karen Marie Moning , *Darkfever*

When selecting texts to encourage visualizing, make sure that students have enough background knowledge to create an image in their minds. For ELL learners, build up a bank of key vocabulary words from the text (with applicable corresponding images) prior to reading the story.

The focus of the lesson is introducing students to the visualizing that happens inside our brains while we read.

Visualizing helps readers comprehend text by forcing their brains to attach images to words. When teaching this strategy, it's important to pick texts that contain strong descriptive language.

Visualizing comes from the same part of our brains as connecting. It's part of that two-way conversation between the reader and the text. Visualizing goes beyond simple imagination, in that the reader uses both his or her background knowledge and the words of the author. We are able to visualize only things that we have experienced or have knowledge about. In this sense, it differs from imagining because it is most often based on or connected to something the reader has experienced. Without a lot of detailed description, it is really hard to visualize something that we have no experience with. I like to talk with students about how we can find images to visualize from the same place in our brain where we find our connections: from our own experiences, other things that we have read or viewed, or things that we have learned about.

It is helpful to introduce the topic of visualizing to students by using a text that is below the grade level they are currently working on. You could use picture books or a short story, or even a short excerpt from a different form of text. Look for stories that are rich in imagery and have strong descriptions. I also find it helpful to select stories where the setting is an integral part of the story. I often use dark or scary stories because they are particularly helpful for discussing mood.

Sequential Lessons for Visualizing

Lesson 1 (Teacher-Directed): Introducing the Power

In this lesson, the teacher models visualizing by sketching his/her vision of what is being read.

- Start with a discussion about what happens in our minds when we read something. Ask students if they have ever been disappointed with how a book was adapted into a film. Most of us have had a favorite book that was turned into a movie: sometimes, the results are all we had hoped; sometimes what we had pictured in our heads is very different from what the director created. Tell students that everyone will picture things slightly differently in their minds because we all have different experiences that make up our schema.
- If your students are totally new to the idea of visualizing, it is helpful to practice visualizing a few common items. For example, ask students to visualize a flower and then have them describe their flower to a partner. Point out that they all have a slightly different image.
- Give the students a nonsense word; e.g., *bandlefrim.* Ask them to visualize it. Their reaction will likely consist of a lot "Huh?"s and "What?"s. This exercise

illustrates the fact that, unless we know about or have a connection to what we are reading, visualizing can be almost impossible to do.

"The Wounded Cormorant" by Liam Flaherty and *Paperboy* by Dav Pilkey are two of my favorite books to use for introducing visualizing because the writing is filled with rich descriptions.

- Select a short piece with strong imagery to practice visualizing.
- Because you need to model the process of visualizing, ask someone else to read the piece out loud. It can be a student or have another adult pop into the room and read.
- While the text is being read, sketch what you are visualizing on the board for students to see.
- After the first read through, ask students if you have missed anything in your drawing. I usually leave out a few important things to elicit student suggestions. If students suggest anything, add it to your sketch.
- Have the reader go through the selection a second time. This time, try to add representations of things picked up by other senses, like sounds, smells, and feelings.
- Again, ask students if you have missed anything and add their suggestions to the sketch.
- Label your sketch with a few key words or picture words.

I like to take a quick picture of the sketch so I can project it onto a screen to use as a reminder for the next lesson.

- Reflect on the fact that while you were drawing you were also making connections, which is what helped you to visualize.
- Tell students that, over the next few lessons, they will practice focusing on images that are communicated through text.

Lesson 2 (Guided Practice): Interacting with the Power

In this lesson, students practice visualizing while the teacher reads a short passage to them.

The focus of this lesson is drawing students' attention to the pictures that are conveyed by the words in the text.

- Remind students of the visual-image sketch you modeled in the previous lesson.
- Hand each student a blank piece of paper. Tell them that you are going to read them a short piece of writing. Say that while you are reading, you would like them to sketch the images that they have in their minds. They can sketch with actual pictures or, if they are uncomfortable with drawing, they can include words that stand out for them in relation to the images.

Point out to students that we all have different strengths, and tell them that the point of this lesson is to get something down on paper and not to see who can create the next masterpiece.

- Read students a short piece or an excerpt from a longer piece of literature, and have them draw and write while you are reading. Depending on the length of the piece, it might be helpful to read the piece two or three times.
- Invite students who are comfortable doing so to share some of the key images from their drawings with the class.

Suggested texts for this lesson include Chapter 8: Flies and Spiders of *The Hobbit* by J.R.R. Tolkien and *Wild Child* by Lynn Plourde.

- After the first reading, ask students to move beyond what they are seeing and add sounds and feelings (mood) on their page. If the piece is short enough, it might be helpful to read through it again to allow students to add detail to their drawings.
- Next, have students share and compare their drawings with a partner. At this point, each pair needs to come up with two ways their drawings are similar and one way their drawings are different. The similarities and differences must focus on content and not just on ability to draw.
- Finally, have a class discussion about what things were common to all drawings. For example, did everyone include certain events or objects in their drawings? What about certain sounds or feelings?
- End the lesson by asking students to reflect on their experience visualizing. Some questions to ask: Did you find visualizing easy? Challenging? How did

it help you understand the text better? Based on the fact that you and your partner had some differences in your drawings, what can you say about how people visualize? Collect student drawings for formative assessment.

> The next lessons deal with the mood or atmosphere of texts. I had a hard time deciding whether to include mood in the visualizing section or in the inferring section. Although mood does require inferring, it is more strongly connected to setting, and therefore to visualizing. I always ask my students to notice how a text makes them feel when they are visualizing. If you feel that mood fits better in the inferring lesson, please feel free to use the following lessons when you are teaching that power instead.

Lesson 3 (Guided Practice): Interacting with the Power

In this lesson, students practice reading the mood of artwork.

- Collect three to five visual images that invoke powerful emotion. One of my favorites is "Stormy Weather on Georgian Bay" by F.H. Varley; note that many paintings by the Group of Seven will work for this activity. Any artwork that invokes feelings will work for this.
- Put up the first piece of artwork so students can see it. Don't give them any information about the work to start.
- Ask students to look at the artwork for a few minutes and to notice what feelings they have while they are looking at it. Ask them to share and record their responses on the board.
- Next, ask students what made them feel this way: maybe it's the colors used; maybe it's the subject of the artwork. Tell students that the way a text or a piece of art makes them feel is called *mood*.
- At this point, it can be helpful to hand out a list of words that could be used to describe mood. See reproducible list on page 44.
- Put up another piece of art and have students write down the title of the piece. Under the title, have students list feelings they have and what makes them feel this way.
- Repeat this step until students have made lists under several titles. Giving students multiple options should allow everyone to find one piece that invokes some emotion for them.
- Invite students to share and compare their mood lists with a partner.
- Finally, have students write a paragraph about the mood of one of the pieces that you viewed in class.
- Collect paragraphs for formative assessment.

Lesson 4 (Guided Practice): Interacting with the Power

In this lesson, students practice sketching images from their minds and expressing feelings invoked from the text.

- Select a grade-level text with a strong sense of mood to read to students.
- Have each student take out a blank piece of paper. Tell them you are going to read them a story and they need to sketch images from their mind. Remind them to focus on the pictures they have in their mind as well as the feelings

that begin to arise for them while they are listening. Remind students that the way the story makes the reader feel is called the mood of the story.

- After you have finished reading, invite students to share their sketches with their shoulder partners (students pair with the person beside them). Remind them to describe to their partner how the story made them feel. Ask them to identify two things in the story that made them feel this way. If either partner is unable to identify where their feelings came from, the other partner can help. If both partners cannot identify where their feelings came from, they can seek out another pair to help them.
- Finally, have each student write a small paragraph describing the mood or feeling of the story. In this paragraph, students need to describe the mood and to identify what part of the story made them feel this way.
- Collect the paragraph for formative assessment.

Lesson 5 (Guided Practice): Interacting with the Power

The focus of this lesson is identifying how setting is connected to understanding.

In this lesson, students practice visualizing and identifying the setting.

- Select a grade-level text with a setting that is an integral part of the story.
- Have students take out a blank piece of paper. Tell students to draw a line across their page about two-thirds of the way down the page. On the top (larger) portion of the paper, students sketch the images and feelings from the story while you read, as they have practiced in the previous lessons. Have them connect their feelings directly to the text. Tell them to leave the bottom (smaller) section for later.
- After reading, give students time to finish their notes and sketches.
- Have students describe the setting on the bottom portion of the paper. They can choose to do this in paragraph or point form.
- Ask students how the story would be different if the setting changed. Ask them why they think the author chose that setting for that story. What kind of information does the setting help communicate? How important is the setting to the story?
- Discuss how the setting of the story affects or enhances our understanding. See if students can make links between what they wrote for setting on the bottom of the page and the images and feelings they sketched on the top of the page. Students can draw actual lines on the page to link ideas.
- End the lesson by asking students to jot down a few points on the back of the paper about how the setting in the story adds to the reader's understanding. Collect papers for formative assessment.

Lesson 6 (Independent Practice): Using the Power

The focus of this lesson is the ability to use visualization to enhance comprehension.

Whenever possible, allow students time for talking and sharing their thinking with others. Oral language helps build comprehension and supports students' written output. When they articulate their thinking, they are better able to write about it.

In this lesson, students apply what they have learned about visualizing in a written paragraph.

- Select a grade-level text to read with students.
- Tell students they may sketch a picture while you read or just make notes about the setting and the mood of the story. When you have finished reading, ask students to share and compare their sketch with a partner, and to talk about similarities and differences between their images.
- After reading the story, have students write a short paragraph describing the setting of the story.

- Next, have students write a second paragraph identifying why the setting is important to the story.
- Finally, provide students with a few alternative settings for the story: e.g., if it takes place in a rural setting, change the setting to a city; if it takes place in the early 1900s, change the setting to present-day. Have them select one of the alternative settings and write a third paragraph describing how the story would be different in that setting.
- Collect paragraphs for summative assessment.

Visualizing	NYM	M	FM	EX
Is able to visualize independently while reading				
Demonstrates an ability to visualize, either through drawing or by oral explanation				
Identifies key images from the story that enhance understanding				
Identifies key words or phrases that prompted visualization of images				
Uses a variety of different senses (sight, sound, taste, etc.) when visualizing				

Focus Literary Device: Setting

While the lessons here focus on recognizing and describing setting, at some point during visualizing lessons it is important to discuss the importance of setting. This will help move students beyond simply telling when and where a story took place and toward being able to discuss why the setting is important to the meaning of the story. The author has chosen the setting for a specific reason; readers need to examine why this setting was chosen and how it influences the reader's understanding of the piece.

SAMPLE LESSON: STORY SETTING

- Select and read with students a story with a strong setting.
- As a class, discuss how the setting contributed to the plot of the story. Talk about the idea that authors select settings for a specific reason.
- Have students create an alternative setting for the story and write a paragraph about how the new setting would affect the plot. For example, how would Romeo and Juliet change if it took place in modern times with cell phones? Would the outcome have changed or would Romeo be stuck in a dead zone with out cell service?

If you can find one, bring a mood ring into the class to introduce mood. It would be a great way to hook kids into the lesson, and helps to illustrate that mood can be different for each reader.

Suggested Story: "The Painted Door" by Sinclair Ross
Discuss: Would the affair have happened if the story was relocated to a city?

Focus Literary Device: Mood

The idea of mood is often difficult for students to grasp, and they often mix up mood and tone. Explain that mood is how the story makes the reader feel and is part of the setting, whereas tone is the attitude the author used when writing the piece. Tone is about the author; mood is about the reader. You can use visualizing lessons to teach students about mood and help them articulate how a piece of literature makes them feel and why it makes them feel that way.

SAMPLE LESSON: SETTING THE MOOD

- Have students create a collage representing the mood of a story. This can be done the traditional way using magazines and paper, or you can have your students create collages online using online photo sites.
- Have students create a poem of found verse out of the parts of the text that helped communicate the mood. The poem can be arranged on top of their collages.

Post the list of mood words on page 44 for quick reference.

Listening to stories told aloud is often helpful to students when they practice visualizing. Radio requires storytellers to use rich imagery in their stories and is a natural fit for practicing visualization. I often use Stuart Mclean's Vinyl Café stories from CBC; you could integrate history into your lessons by using classic radio dramas like *War of the Worlds* by Orson Welles.

Prompts and Sentence Frames to Encourage Visualizing

- Describe the setting. Draw a picture of what you just read in the text.
- *The setting affected the story because…*
- What techniques does the author use to create a picture in your mind (descriptive language, simile, metaphor, hyperbole, imagery)? Find an example of each technique in the text.
- Pick three colors to represent three different parts of the text. Describe why you picked each color and how it represents that part of the text.
- Describe the mood of the text. How does the author communicate this mood?
- Describe the tone of the text. How does the author communicate this tone?
- Imagine this text was made into a movie or TV show, and you were in charge of selecting the location for filming; describe the location you would choose.
- How did the reading make you feel? What made you feel that way?
- If you changed one aspect of the setting, how would the story change?
- Describe three images that stuck in your mind as you were reading.

Books listed are appropriate for use with high-school students. Those that could also be used in middle-school classes are marked with an M.

Suggested Texts for Visualizing

"Trapped in the Desert" by Gary Beeman (short story, M)

Three Day Road by Joseph Boyden (novel; strong content)

"Swimming Upstream" by Beth Brant (short story)

"Jabberwocky" by Lewis Carroll (poem, M)

"Kubla Khan" by Samuel Taylor Coleridge (poem)

Come On, Rain! by Karen Hesse (picture book, M)

"A Sunrise on the Veldt" by Doris Lessing (short story, M)

The Specific Ocean by Kyo Maclear (picture book, M)

Josepha: A Prairie Boy's Story by Jim McGugan (picture book, M)

"The Highway Man" by Alfred Noyes (poem, M)

"The Wounded Cormorant" by Liam O'Flaherty (short story, M)

Paperboy by Dav Pilkey (picture book, M)

Wild Child by Lynn Plourde (picture book, M)

"The Shark" by E.J. Pratt (poem, M)

"The Painted Door" by Sinclair Ross (short story)

Sonnet 130 by William Shakespeare (poem)

Heatwave by Eileen Spinelli (picture book, M)

"Ashes for the Wind" by Hernando Tellez (short story)

"Do Not Go Gentle into that Good Night" by Dylan Thomas (poem)

"Chapter 8: Flies and Spiders" *The Hobbit* by J.R.R. Tolkien (novel excerpt, M)

Owl Moon by Jane Yolen (picture book, M)

Words Describing Mood

aggravated	hyper
amused	irritated
angry	joyful
annoyed	lonely
anxious	mellow
blissful	nervous
calm	optimistic
cheerful	peaceful
content	relaxed
cranky	relieved
depressed	restless
distressed	scared
energetic	sentimental
excited	silly
exhilarated	sympathetic
gloomy	terrified
grumpy	thankful
happy	thoughtful
harmonious	uncomfortable
hopeful	worried
hopeless	

5 Questioning

"I think kids want the same thing from a book that adults want — a fast-paced story, characters worth caring about, humor, surprises, and mystery. A good book always keeps you asking questions, and makes you keep turning pages so you can find out the answers." — Rick Riordan

Our older students, depending on their experiences in the earlier grades, may have rarely been asked to think about what they are wondering while they are reading a text. I'm sure many of them had experience with the K–W–L (Know–Wonder–Learn) chart or its many cousins, but that was just a pre-reading activity that happened before the real learning began. We ask them to answer questions or summarize after they have finished reading, but rarely ask them what questions are in their heads during the actual process of reading.

Proficient readers ask questions while they read. These questions help the reader check for understanding, realize when they are confused, and fill in the blanks when something is unclear. When followed by inferences (see chapter 6) these questions also help to enhance understanding of the text.

It is often effective to introduce this reading power with a discussion about the different kinds of questions that students have been asked about the literature that they read. At this point, they all have some experience (sometimes too much experience!) with all levels of questions. Students are probably most familiar with literal hunt-and-find questions, for which they have to scan through the text, looking for the one correct answer. Most have encountered the dreaded *What do you think…?* or its cousin *Why do you think…?* questions on assignments and tests. Since these questions do not have one correct answer, they are often the ones that students struggle with.

Consider following up on this introduction with a conversation about how students feel when characters in books and movies do things readers and viewers aren't expecting them to do. Most of us have had the experience of asking ourselves, *Why did he/she do that?* in response to the actions of a character; examining this experience is a good way to get students thinking about questioning as a strategy for reading and viewing.

Sequential Lessons for Questioning

Lesson 1 (Teacher-Directed): Introducing the Power

The focus of this lesson is modeling questioning while reading.

I like to use *Sparrow Girl* by Sarah Pennypacker or "The Veldt" by Ray Bradbury.

In this lesson, students record the teacher's questions before, during, and after the reading of a text.

- Select a grade-level text to read with students. Pre-read the passage and jot down both literal and inferential questions ahead of time so that you are modeling different types of questions for students.
- Tell students that you are going to share some questions about the text that are going through your mind while you are reading. Explain that these are questions that would normally be going on inside your head but that you are asking them aloud because you want the students to hear your thinking.

See page 52 for the Question Chart.

- Ask students to draw three columns on a piece of paper and write the headings *Before*, *During*, and *After* at the top (or use the Question Chart on page 52). While you are reading, they will write down the questions that you share.
- Read the title of the story and any background information you have. Share a few questions that you have about the story before you read. Try to use the frame "I'm wondering..." Students will record one or two of these questions in the first column on their paper.
- Begin reading the story with students, pausing a few times to share your questions as you read. Remind students that they are writing down your questions in the middle column as you share.
- Finish reading the story. Explain that good readers often think about a story, even after it's finished. Share out any questions that you still have after reading. Try to use the frame "I'm still wondering..."
- Once students have finished recording your questions in all three columns, ask them to read over the questions to see which ones have already been answered. Some of your earlier literal questions might well have been answered, while some others might still be unknown. Ask students to record the answer next to any questions that have been addressed in the text.

This discussion will set the stage for later lessons around questions that clarify and questions that extend thinking.

- End the lesson by talking to students about the value of asking questions when they read. Have them discuss with a partner why they think it's important to use this strategy. Explain that sometimes asking questions that don't have answers can extend the reader's thinking and understanding.

Lesson 2 (Guided Practice): Interacting with the Power

In this lesson, students practice asking before-, during-, and after-reading questions.

The focus of this lesson is how different questions have different purposes.

- Begin the lesson:

  Do you have one friend you hate watching movies with because he/she always asks questions?

  After a few laughs, ask students why that friend asks so many questions. Students will likely come up with the answer that the purpose of questions is to clarify understanding.
- Ask students if they ever ask questions about what they are reading. Many will never have thought about it; however, after a little prompting, most will offer that they have had the experience of asking "Why did he/she do that?" or "I wonder if this is going to happen?"

For this lesson, I would recommend "All the Troubles of the World" by Isaac Asimov and *If* by Sarah Perry.

- Pass out a few sticky notes to each student. Tell them that while you read a story, you would like them to jot down any questions that come to mind; they should write one question per sticky note.
- Read the title of the story that you have selected and give students a bit of background on the story or author. Ask them to write down one thing they are wondering about the story just from the title (and/or the cover, if you are using a picture book) and the background. Tell them that these are called *before-reading questions*, and that these questions help us focus our thinking on the text you are about to read.
- Begin reading the story. You might choose to pause a few times during the reading to allow students time to write down another question or two. Tell them that the questions they are writing are called *during-reading questions*.

Explain that during-reading questions help our brains sort information and check for understanding.

- At the end of the story, have them write down one or two things about which they are still wondering. Tell students that these are *after-reading questions*, and that they are used to extend our thinking and to check for understanding. Ask them how they feel about stories that end suddenly without explaining what happened to all of the characters. Most will probably have a strong reaction about how unsettled unresolved stories leave us feeling.
- Starting with the before-reading questions, have willing students share out. Record a few questions on the board. Then have a few students share out the during-reading questions they have. Finally, have a few students share out the after-reading questions they have. Continue to record their questions on the board.
- Lead students through a discussion of what kinds of questions were asked at each different time. See if they can identify *focusing questions* (beginning), *clarifying questions* (during), and *extending questions* (after). While not all questions will fit this format, enough should correspond to it to help illustrate the power of asking different types of questions.
- End the lesson by having students reflect on how asking questions can help the reader to better understand a piece of text. They can discuss with a partner and/or write a short reflection. Collect sticky notes for formative assessment and the next lesson.

Lesson 3 (Guided Practice): Interacting with the Power

The focus of this lesson is how questions help focus, clarify, and extend the reader's thinking.

In this lesson, students are challenged to identify when questions from the previous lesson were asked; i.e., at the beginning, middle, or end of the story.

- Create and head three categories on the board: *Before-reading questions*, *During-reading questions*, and *After-reading questions*. See if students can remember the different purposes of the three questions. Record the purposes of the questions under each heading: focusing, clarifiying, extending.
- Using sticky notes from the previous lesson, read through some of the questions with students. See if they can identify when a question was asked by the type of information it is asking. Some questions might fit under more than one category so, if students are brave enough to own up to their own questions, they can tell when the question was asked. If students don't want to identify their questions, the class can make a decision about what category each question belongs in.
- After the share-out and sort, have students select the most important example question from the lesson. On a piece of paper, they will record their selected question and give one reason why they think this question was important to the reader's understanding.
- Collect their writing for formative assessment.

Lesson 4 (Guided Practice): Interacting with the Power

The focus of this lesson is noticing the difference between *literal* or *quick* questions and *inferential* or *deep-thinking* questions.

In this lesson, students practice using questioning before, during, and after reading.

- On a piece of paper, have students write down the headings *Before-reading*, *During-reading*, and *After-reading*, leaving room in between each heading (or use the Question Chart on page 52).

See page 52 for the Question Chart.

Here's another way to categorize questions:

Snorkel questions: literal questions that skim the surface of the story; answers found directly in the text. Scuba questions: questions that dive deep into the meaning of the story; answers are not found in the text but extend and enhance understanding. Cloud questions: questions that float away from the meaning of the text; answers are not found in the text, but often don't make a difference to your understanding.

If using a story that you have used in your class before, or one that comes with a teacher's guide with a list of questions, you can hand out existing questions to students and have them decide which are literal questions and which are inferential questions.

The focus of this lesson is illustrating that thinking doesn't need to stop just because the reader is finished the text.

- Introduce students to the title and author of the grade-level text you will read to them. Give them time to write down one or two questions under the *Before-reading* heading.
- Tell students that, while you are reading, they will write down any questions they have under the *During-reading* heading. Begin reading the story to them, pausing a few times to give them a chance to jot down their questions.
- At the end of the story, have students write down a few questions they are still wondering about under the *After-reading* heading.
- Put a two-column chart on the whiteboard with the headings *Literal/Quick Questions* and *Inferential/Deep-thinking Questions*.
- Talk about how literal (quick) questions are questions that are answered directly by the author, and for which the answer can be found directly in the text. Discuss how inferential (deep-thinking) questions require the author and the reader to develop an answer based on their own thinking, since it cannot be found directly in the text.
- Hand out two sticky notes to each student and have them write their two favorite questions on them, one per sticky note. Have students bring their sticky notes up to the front of the classroom and place them in the columns where they think they fit.
- Read over the questions as a group and decide if they are in the correct column. See if students can remember what kinds of questions are usually asked before, during, and after reading. If possible, have them guess when some of the questions were asked, based on the information being sought.
- Have each student select five questions to answer on a piece of paper. Encourage them to select questions from both columns, but keep in mind that some students may not be able to answer inferential questions if they have not been taught how.
- End the lesson by having students share their favorite question and answer with a partner. Collect papers for formative assessment.

Lesson 5 (Guided Practice): Interacting with the Power

In this lesson, students practice asking *What if…?* questions to extend their thinking.

- Select a grade-level text to read with students.
- Have students create a three-column chart on a piece of paper for their before-reading, during-reading, and after-reading questions.
- Give students the title of the text and a bit of background information about the text and the author. Allow some time for them to record before-reading questions.
- Read the text with students, pausing a few times during reading to allow them to write their during-reading questions.
- At the end of the piece, allow students a few moments to write down their after-reading questions.
- Do a quick review of Lesson 4 on literal and inferential questions (page 47). Write the categories *Literal Questions* and *Inferential Questions* on the board and see if students can remember the difference between the two types of questions. Have a few students share out their questions and see if students can sort them.
- Introduce students to the *What if…?* question. *What if the main character had made a different decision? What if Juliet had married Paris? What if the story*

had been told by the antagonist? Brainstorm a list of *What if…?* questions with students. All these questions belong under the Inferential Questions heading because the answer requires information both from the author and from readers' thinking.

- End the lesson by having each student select a favorite *What if…?* question and write a paragraph about how the story would have changed if the *What if* had become a reality.
- Collect writing for formative assessment.

Lesson 6 (Independent Practice): Using the Power

In this lesson, students apply what they have learned about questions and write a letter to the author of the text.

The focus of this lesson is students demonstrating their ability to use before-, during-, and after-reading questions to guide their thinking.

See page 52 for the Question Chart.

- Have students take out a piece of paper and write down three headings: *Before-reading*, *During-reading*, and *After-reading*. Or hand out the Question Chart on page 52.
- Select a grade-level text to read with students; give them the title, author, and a bit of background information about the text. Have them write down their before-reading questions to help focus their thinking.
- Read the text with students, pausing a few times to give them time to write down during-reading questions.
- At the end of the story, have students write down after-reading questions that they are still wondering about.
- Have students go back and look over their questions to see if any of them were answered during the reading. If they were answered, have them jot down the answers beside the question.
- Tell students that they are going to write a letter to the author of the text about the questions the reading prompted.

This lesson could fit nicely in a writing unit on letters or e-mail. Students could send their letters to the author, if possible.

- You can give students some ideas for framing their letter. Suggest that the first paragraph could start with the sentence, "At first, I was wondering …."; their second paragraph could start "During the story I was wondering about …"; their final paragraph could start with "Now that I have finished the story, I am still wondering …" Remind students to include any answers to their questions.
- Collect charts and letters for summative assessment.

Key

NYM = Not Yet Meeting
M = Meeting
FM = Fully Meeting
EX = Exceeding

Asking Questions	NYM	M	FM	EX
Is able to generate questions independently while reading				
Demonstrates an understanding of the difference between quick (literal), deep-thinking (thoughtful, relevant), and not-connected (not relevant to meaning of the story) questions				
Is able to independently generate questions that enhance understanding and are directly related to the meaning of the text				
Is able to answer both literal and inferential questions using information from the text and own thinking to enhance understanding				

Is able to explain how a question has led to better understanding of the text				

Focus Literary Device: Plot and Conflict

There are basic questions that revolve around the main events occurring in any story. Often these student-generated questions are literal and focus on the plot. (*Why did he/she do that? What is going to happen to him/her? What's going to happen next?*) You can focus on these basic questions to create story maps of the rising action, climax, and falling action.

The second most-basic type of question in every story revolves around the conflict and how it gets resolved. Questioning lessons are a great time to review the types of conflict with students. *Is this story about a conflict between two people or groups of people? Is this story about an internal conflict between a person and him or herself? Is this a story about the struggle between a person and the environment?*

Sample Lesson: From Questions to Plot Diagram

Build a plot diagram with students as you read through a story. Once you have identified plot points, have students develop a list of questions related to the points.

- You could have them focus on "I wonder if… if…" questions; e.g., *I wonder if Jack would have fallen if Jill had led the way down the hill.* These types of questions set the stage for inferring.
- Rather than simply having students identify the conflict in a text, have them turn the conflict into an "I wonder…" question: e.g., *I wonder if Macbeth will give in to Lady Macbeth's pressure? I wonder how the conflict between the Montagues and the Capulets will affect the romance between Romeo and Juliet?* As an extension, students could then brainstorm a list of answers to their conflict question and write a paragraph or essay response.

This is a great way to review plot structure and to give students a concrete visual of how the types of questions that we ask tend to change as we move through the text.

Prompts and Sentence Frames to Encourage Questioning

- *Before reading, I was wondering…*
- *During reading, I was wondering…*
- *After reading, I wonder…*
- *This text made me wonder about…*
- *I wonder what would happen if the author changed the…*
- If the author were here, what three questions would you ask about the text?
- If one of the characters were here, what three questions would you ask that character?
- What are three questions that were answered by the end of the text?
- What are three questions that were not answered by the end of the text? How does this increase your enjoyment of the text?
- What is the main conflict in the story? Are there any secondary conflicts?

Books listed are appropriate for use with high-school students. Those that could also be used in middle-school classes are marked with an M.

Suggested Texts for Questioning

"All the Troubles of the World" by Isaac Asimov (short story)

"Frustration" by Isaac Asimov (short story)

Oryx and Crake by Margaret Atwood (novel)

The Compound by S.A. Bodeen (novel, M)

"The Veldt" by Ray Bradbury (short story, M)

Fly Away Home by Eve Bunting (picture book, M)

"If I Forget Thee, Oh Earth…" by Arthur C. Clarke (short story)

"Mirror Image" by Lena Coakley (short story)

"Mother to Son" by Langston Hughes (poem, M)

Invitation to the Game by Monica Hughes (novel)

"The Lottery" by Shirley Jackson (short story, M)

"The Monkey's Paw" by W.W. Jacobs (short story, M)

"Totem" by Thomas King (short story)

The Stamp Collector by Jennifer Lauthier (picture book, M)

Phileas's Fortune by Agnes de Lestrade (picture book, M)

Every Day by David Levithan (novel)

If You Find Me by Emily Murdoch (novel)

Sparrow Girl by Sara Pennypacker (picture book, M)

If by Sarah Perry (picture book, M)

"The Tell-tale Heart" by Edgar Allan Poe (short story, M)

"A Bolt of White Cloth" by Leon Rooke (short Story)

An Angel for Solomon Simon by Cynthia Rylant (picture book, M)

The Composition by Antonio Skarmeta (picture book, M)

Mr. Bear and the Bear by Frances Thomas (picture book, M)

A Man Called Raven by Richard van Camp (picture book, M)

"The Street that Got Mislaid" by Patrick Waddington (short story, M)

Question Chart

	I am wondering… (question)	because… (what makes me wonder that)
Before Reading		
During Reading		
After Reading		

Pembroke Publishers © 2016 *Powerful Readers* by Kyla Hadden and Adrienne Gear ISBN 978-1-55138-313-2

6 Inferring

Inferring is the bedrock of comprehension, not only in reading. We infer in many realms. Our life clicks along more smoothly if we can read the world as well as text (Harvey and Goudvis, 2007, page 138)

I like to introduce older students to the idea of denotation and connotation. Denotation is the dictionary definition of the words, or the literal meaning. Connotation is the cultural or emotional meaning of the words, or the figurative meaning. When inferring, you need to understand the denotation of the words, but most of the meaning is found in the connotation of the words.

Inferring, or reading between the lines, can be a difficult concept for some students to understand. A quick dictionary search for the term *infer* produces words such as "evidence," "deduce," "conclude," and "implicit." The last word, *implicit*, is central to the idea of inferring. The author implies something through words rather than explicitly telling the reader that thing. Post a definition for *inferring* somewhere prominent in the classroom and refer to this definition often as you work through the inferring lessons.

We often ask our students "What did the author mean when he/she wrote this?" When we ask students this question, what we are really asking them to do is to infer what the author meant. Any time we ask students to comment on anything that is not directly written in the text, we are asking them to infer. Any time an author uses figurative language, they are asking the reader to infer. Anytime teachers ask students the dreaded *Why do you think…?* question, they are asking the students to infer. If we are asking our students to infer, which we do quite often, we need to make sure that we are actually teaching them what it is and how to do it.

There is a strong link between inferring and the other Reading Power strategies. If readers cannot make connections between their own experiences and the author's words, they will not be able to infer. For example, if readers have no experience with how people look and act when they are angry, they will not be able to make inferences about why a character storms out of the room after an argument. When authors use figurative language, they are relying on most readers having the background knowledge to make sense of their implications.

There is also a strong link between inferring and questioning. Students who have been taught to ask deep-thinking questions when they read are, in fact, preparing to infer. When readers attempt to answer a deep-thinking question, using "I think…" or "Maybe…," they are, in fact, inferring. As I teach this strategy, I like to tell students that good writers leave spaces for our thinking. It's our job, as active readers, to pay attention to those spaces and to add our *maybe*s into the text.

Begin the inferring lessons by pointing out that we make inferences every day. Ask students to tell about times when they have had to use inferring in their everyday life. Most of us have had to infer people's feelings or emotions based on their behaviors. Many teenagers have probably waited until they knew a parent was in a good mood before asking for something. Ask students how they know that a friend, parent, or boy/girlfriend is in a good mood. It might be helpful to look out the window and make an inference about what it is like outside right now; e.g., "I infer that it is muggy outside right now because it was raining and now it is sunny." This helps solidify the idea that inferences are more than just random guesses; inferences are educated guesses supported by evidence.

When inferring while reading, inferences require information from the text and thinking from the reader. You can present this in the form of an equation:

Evidence from the text + Reader's thoughts = Inferring

Sequential Lessons for Inferring

Lesson 1 (Teacher-Directed): Introducing the Power

The focus of this lesson is the idea that inferences are educated guesses supported by facts.

In this lesson, the teacher uses short scenarios to model inferring. Tell students that you are going to make some inferences, or educated guesses, about what is happening in short scenarios.

- Read the following scenario to students:

  Jill stormed into the room and slammed the door behind her. Her face was bright red and her fists were clenched.

- Ask students to talk with a partner about what they think might be happening, how Jill might be feeling, and any connections they might have to Jill.
- Tell students that you infer that Jill was angry about something because her face was red, her fists were clenched, and she slammed the door. Because you have experienced anger before, you can make an educated guess based on her physical behavior.
- Read the next scenario to students:

  The lights dimmed and a hush fell over the crowd. Lee grabbed a handful of popcorn and shoved it in his mouth. It was about to begin.

- Invite students to turn and talk about what they infer and any connections they have to this scenario.
- Tell students that you infer that Lee is at the movies because the lights just dimmed and he's eating popcorn. Because you have been to the movies before, you can make an educated guess based on the description.
- Read the next scenario to students:

  Adam carefully pushed his toes to the edge of the platform. He grabbed the safety harness, suddenly questioning it's strength. The instructor began the countdown.

Writing Extension: Give students a scenario: e.g., *a person is just about to walk on stage to give a speech to the school*. Have them write 2–3 sentences describing the scene without revealing the actual event.

- Ask students if they can make any inferences about what is happening. They will probably suggest bungee jumping or skydiving. Ask them what clues they used to infer what was happening.
- Tell students that, over the next few lessons, they will practice inferring while they read and view things.

Lesson 2 (Guided Practice): Interacting with the Power

The focus of this lesson is noticing how our own thinking can combine with facts to create inferences.

In this lesson, students are introduced to inferring through photographs.

- For this lesson, you will need a collection of pictures of people. Look for ones in which the subject is showing obvious emotion. I suggest three or four pictures to examine as a class, and then one picture for every two or three students for the second part of the lesson.

- Remind students how, in the previous lesson, they practiced making inferences about short scenarios using clues in the text. Explain that in this lesson they will be practicing making inferences again, but this time they will be using clues from pictures.
- Display the first picture for students to see. Ask them to describe the person in the picture; record their responses on the board. Look for obvious descriptors, such as hair color, eye color, and gender, but also encourage less obvious descriptors, such as emotions or feelings. For example, when looking at photographs students might make statements such as "She is happy," based on the subject's expression.
- Once students have suggested a variety of descriptors, ask them to sort the list into two groups: things they know for sure, like hair color and eye color, and things they think they are inferring from something in the picture, like feelings based on the person's facial expression. Tell students that this is the difference between direct information and inferring.
- Repeat the process with a few more pictures. Encourage students to use language such as "I think" or "maybe" in their inferences. Also, remind students that their inferences must always be backed up with evidence. Any *I think* statement needs to be followed by a *because…* explanation. For example, *I think he is angry because his brows are scrunched and his arms are crossed.*
- Finally, divide students up into groups of two or three. Give a hard copy of a new picture to each group. On the back of the picture, have students write the headings *Things I Know for Sure* and *Inferences*.
- In groups, students examine their photos and record information under each heading. Once again, remind students that their inferences must be followed by evidence to support the inference.
- Collect photos for formative assessment.

Lesson 3 (Guided Practice): Interacting with the Power

The focus of the lesson is supporting inferences with evidence.

The website gocomics.com is a great source to access a variety of short comics. Farside cartoons are also great for practicing inferring.

For this lesson, I recommend "Message in a Bottle" by Rodolphe Guenoden.

In this lesson, students practice inferring using comic strips. Comics and cartoons are a great way to introduce inferring because they don't contain a lot of text and they require the reader to infer a lot based on clues and facial expressions. In addition, comic strips often leave gaps between the frames where readers must fill in events. I always tell my students that less text from the writer means more thinking from the reader. The less text, the better for inferring.

- Hand out a hard copy of a detailed comic to each student. If you can, project the comic so that you can refer to specific points with the class.
- Tell students you are going to give them a few minutes to look over the comic to figure out what is happening. Ask them to write their ideas directly on the paper. Encourage them to draw lines connecting their ideas to specific points in the text. Remind them to list the direct evidence (things they can actually see) and their inferences (what they are thinking about).
- Once students have had a few minutes to interact with the comic, begin a discussion about what is happening in the piece. Each time a student provides a piece of information, ask them "How do you know that is true?" Students need to back up their inferences with evidence from the text or with their background knowledge. Tell them that if they don't have evidence to support their inferences, then it is not an inference. You can have students put a line through anything they cannot support with evidence.
- Encourage students to record inferences from their classmates if they agree with them or didn't think of them on their own.

- End the lesson by having students explain the difference between an inference and a guess. They can do this by discussing with a partner and/or by writing a short reflection. Collect student copies for formative assessment.

Lesson 4 (Guided Practice): Interacting with the Power

The focus of this lesson is supporting inferences with evidence from the text.

In this lesson, students practice making inferences using text-based pieces.

- Find a grade-level text to read with students. Recommended texts include "The Necklace" by Guy Maupassant or *This Is Not My Hat* by Jon Klassen.
- Before you read, review the idea of inferring with students. Remind them that an inference is more than just a guess about something in the text; it is a thought backed up by information from the text and our connections.
- Write the phrase *I think… because…* on the board. Tell students that they will need to use this sentence frame to write three inferences about the story you are about to read. You might want to hand out sticky notes for students to write their inferences on. That way, they can put their inferences right beside the text that helped them make that inference.
- Read the story with students, pausing a few times to direct them toward obvious places for inferences. For example, you could ask "Does anyone have an inference about how _____ is feeling right now?" or "Why do you think _____ reacted this way?"
- Once you have finished reading the text, ask students to share out a few of their inferences. Record them on the board, making sure students are using the sentence frame that you provided at the beginning of the lesson. This will help model the process for students that might still be struggling with it.
- Have each student select his or her favorite *I think… because…* inference. They can share their favorite inference with a partner and/or write a reflection. Collect written reflections for formative assessment.

Lesson 5 (Guided Practice): Interacting with the Power

The focus of this lesson is practicing supporting inferences with evidence.

In this lesson, students complete a chart connecting their inferences directly back to the text.

See page 61 for reproducible chart; see sample on page 57 for "A Kind of Murder."

Sometimes our inferences are derived more from our background knowledge and connections than from the text. For example, if in the story Jonny has a fight with his best friend, many of us would be able to infer that Jonny would be upset or angry, even without clues from the author. I think it's important to recognize background knowledge as evidence. Students should still be able to identify the place in the text where the inference happened, but their evidence may come more from their own experiences.

- Find a grade-level text to read with students. I recommend "A Kind of Murder" by Hugh Pentecost.
- Before reading, create a two-column chart with the headings *Text Support* and *Inference*.
- Provide students with at least one example of an inference from the text you are using. Remind them that an inference is something you believe to be true based on something from the text. Provide students with an example of an inference; see sample on page 57.
- Tell students that, while you are reading, they will record on their chart their inferences and the piece of text (quote or description of event) that led them to the inference. Pause a few times while reading the text to allow students time to write down their thoughts. If you can provide them with a photocopy of the story, they can record their emerging thoughts directly on the paper and complete the chart at the end of the story.
- At the end of the lesson, have students share out their inferences. Encourage polite debate about any responses that are not true inferences. Remind students that, if the response was directly communicated by the author, even if it is important for comprehension, it is not an inference. If the students cannot

back up their response with text support (or background knowledge), it is not an inference.

- Collect the charts for formative assessment.

SAMPLE INFERRING CHART: "A KIND OF MURDER" BY HUGH PENTECOST

Text Support	Inference
He shows up to check on him part-way through the night.	Old Beaver doesn't think that Mr. Warren can handle the boys in study hall on the first night.
	Mr. Warren likes animals.

Lesson 6 (Guided Practice): Interacting with the Power

The focus of this lesson is supporting inferences with evidence from the text.

In this lesson, students examine other students' inferences and try to identify the evidence from the text.

- Select a grade-level text to read with students.
- Before you read, tell students that they will be writing down five inferences from the text and recording the part of the text that led them to make each inference.
- Read the text with students, pausing a few times to allow students to record their inferences and evidence from the text to support them.
- At the end of the text, tell students to write their inferences on a new piece of paper, but to leave out where the inference came from. If students have inferences that came from their background knowledge, they need to write *Personal Inference* beside the inference. This will give partners a clue that they need to look inside themselves for the evidence to support this inference.
- Once everyone has recorded their inferences on a new piece of paper, have students trade papers with a partner. Tell students that they must try to find the part of the text that supports each inference made by their partner. Students will need time to read back through the text to find the evidence to support their partner's inferences.
- Once students have had a chance to write down their answers, invite them to go over their findings with their partner to see if they were able to identify the piece of text that supports each inference.
- End the lesson by discussing this activity. How easy was it to find the evidence from someone else's inference compared to their own? Was it difficult to support inferences that came from someone's background knowledge? Collect papers for formative assessment.

Lesson 7 (Independent Practice): Using the Power

The focus of this lesson is applying the comprehension strategy of inferring.

In this lesson, students demonstrate their ability to make inferences and support them with evidence from the lesson.

- Select a grade-level text to read with students.
- Tell students that, while you are reading, they will write down inferences they have about the story. Remind them that each inference requires text support. They need to communicate what part of the text made them believe that piece of information to be true.

- You might choose to hand out sticky notes so that students can stick their inferences next to the text that provided them with that piece of information.
- Read through the text with students, pausing a few times during the reading to allow students time to record their thoughts.
- At the end of the story, have students write a paragraph titled "Things I Believe to be True." In this paragraph, they will communicate their inferences as well as the text support for them.
- Collect paragraphs for summative assessment.

Making Inferences	NYM	M	FM	EX
Is able to make simple inferences from a picture or photo				
Uses background knowledge and experiences **plus** clues from the text to support inference.				
Can tell at least two things not written or shown in the text and give reasons with little or no support				
Uses the language of thinking without prompting; e.g. *Maybe…, I think…, It could be…, It's because…, Perhaps…, It means that…*				

Focus Literary Device: Direct and Indirect Characterization

Good readers are able to infer things about characters based on information that is not directly provided by the author. The inferring lesson provides an excellent opportunity for a conversation about direct and indirect characterization. Direct characterization is the information about the character that is provided by the author. Indirect characterization is the information that the reader infers based on a character's actions, words, and thoughts.

Sample Lesson: Characterization

See page 62 for the Characterization chart.

- Have students pick one main character from a story.
- Provide each student with a two-column chart with the headings *Direct Characterization* and *Indirect Characterization*.
- Under *Direct Characterization*, have students record any information about the character that is provided directly by the author. This usually includes things like physical description. Students should quote the text that provides the direct characterization beside each point on the list.
- Under *Indirect Characterization*, have students record any information they can infer about the character using the text and their own thoughts. This usually includes things such as character traits. Again, students should record the text that provides the indirect characterization beside each point on the list.
- Once students have completed the chart, have them write a character sketch of the character. Younger students should be encouraged to connect their inferences back to the text through description. Older students can be encouraged to use direct quotes in their writing to support their thinking.

Focus Literary Device: Figurative Language

Authors often use figurative language, such as metaphors, similes, hyperbole, symbolism, and allusion, to indirectly convey information to the reader. All of these techniques require the reader to infer information based on the author's choice of words and can be included as part of the inferring lessons.

Sample Lesson: Figurative Language

- Find a story or poem that is rich in figurative language. I recommend the poem "History Lesson" by Jeannette Armstrong.
- Go through the text and highlight all the figurative language used in the text. Depending on your students' understanding of figurative language techniques, you could do this for students, or you could work as a group to identify the different techniques.
- Create a two-column chart with all the examples that you have highlighted recorded in the left column of the chart. In the right column, leave room for students to record their thinking around what the author meant by each use of figurative language.
- End the lesson by discussing how figurative language techniques add meaning to text.
- Collect the charts for formative assessment.

My teaching around figurative language used to centre on having students memorize the definitions of the various literary techniques. After that, I would see if they could identify the techniques in stories and poems, and maybe have them write a few. That was it! We rarely talked about how figurative language added to the meaning of the text.

Prompts and Sentence Frames to Encourage Inferring

- *I think… because…*
- *Although the author doesn't directly say it, I infer that…*
- Describe the personality of one of the main characters. What clues did the author give to make you think this?
- Predict what will happen next. What makes you think this?
- Pick an event in the text and describe how you think the characters felt about that event. What made you think this?
- Describe what motivates a character to behave the way they do.
- Describe three things that you believe to be true about the text. What made you believe these things?
- Find three examples of how the author communicates something without directly telling the reader. For each inference, describe how the author communicates it.
- Think back to questions you had while reading that were not answered by the text. Infer an answer to those questions.
- Compare and contrast how two different characters feel about an event that happened in the text.

Books listed are appropriate for use with high-school students. Those that could also be used in middle-school classes are marked with an M.

Suggested Texts for Inferring

"History Lesson" by Jeannette Armstrong (poem)

Mirror by Jeannie Baker (picture book, M)

"Hunger" by Laurence Binyon (poem, M)

"Five Ways to Kill a Man" by Edwin Brock (poem, M)

Voices in the Park by Anthony Browne (picture book, M)

"My Last Duchess" by Robert Browning (poem)

Underground: Finding the Light to Freedom by Shane Evans (picture book, M)

"Words to a Grandchild" by Chief Dan George (poem)

"Message in a Bottle" by Rodolphe Guenoden (graphic short story, M)

"Song: To Celia" by Ben Jonson (poem)

This Is Not My Hat by Jon Klassen (picture book, M)

"The Necklace" by Guy de Maupassant (short story)

"A Kind of Murder" by Hugh Pentecost (short story, M)

Why? by Nikolai Popov (picture book, M)

Yo! Yes! by Chris Raschka (picture book, M)

"Two Girls of Twelve ..." by Charles Reznikoff (poem, M)

"Richard Cory" by Edwin Arlington Robinson (poem)

"Alicia" by Gabrielle Roy (short story, M)

"Rock Bottom" by Steven Keewatin Sanderson (graphic short story)

Butter Battle Book by Dr. Seuss (picture book, M)

"All the World's A Stage" in *As You Like It* by William Shakespeare (monologue)

Hamlet by William Shakespeare (play)

Macbeth by William Shakespeare (play)

Maus I by Art Spiegelman (graphic novel, M)

Maus II by Art Speigelman (graphic novel, M)

Of Mice and Men by John Steinbeck (novel)

The Arrival by Shaun Tan (graphic novel)

The Red Tree by Shaun Tan (picture book, M)

Rules of Summer by Shaun Tan (picture book, M)

The Mysteries of Harris Burdick by Chris Van Allsburg (picture book, M)

Flotsam by David Weisner (picture book, M)

"The Metaphor" by Budge Wilson (short story, M)

Inferring Chart

Text Support	Inference

Pembroke Publishers © 2016 *Powerful Readers* by Kyla Hadden and Adrienne Gear ISBN 978-1-55138-313-2

Characterization

Direct Characterization	Indirect Characterization

7 Transforming

"What is wonderful about great literature is that it transforms the man who reads it towards the condition of the man who wrote."
— E.M. Forster, *Two Cheers for Democracy*

Transforming builds on all the other four Reading Power strategies. A piece of text cannot transform the reader if the reader cannot make connections, use visual imagery, ask questions, and make inferences. True transforming requires readers to recognize their own understandings before reading, combine these understandings with the text during reading, and create an altered understanding after reading.

To transform something means to change it into something new. Simply put, certain texts have the power to transform us by changing our views about ourselves, about others, or about the world. You need only walk into the Self-help section of a library or bookstore to see hundreds of books intended to change our thinking or our actions in some way. We still keep parts of our old views, but our world is slightly changed by something we read. Sometimes, we won't see a change in our thinking, but a text might serve to reinforce thoughts that we already have. Sometimes books have a way of lingering in our thinking, mingling with thoughts we already had, and slowly changing the way we look at something.

In high-school, transformation is also sometimes known as *synthesis*. Powerful readers are able to take the text, mix it with their own thoughts and beliefs, and create a new thought. Sometimes the term *new thought* is misleading: it does not necessarily mean a brand new thought coming out of thin air. When explaining this strategy to students, I like using the term "thinking adjustment" rather than "new thought."

Students quite often think that only nonfiction text can teach the reader something about the world. Transformed thinking, however, goes beyond adding new information into our bank of knowledge. It is the combination of information we read with information or thinking we already have. Fiction allows the reader to experience life lessons without actually having the experience. Think back to the stories and novels that you have read in your lifetime. How many of these books are centred around tough themes, such as death, loss, or failure? Adults may, in fact, have had direct experience with these themes. For teenagers, whose life experiences may be more limited, literature provides a medium for exploring tough concepts and ideas in a safe place. Literature allows them to experience the lives of characters that may be completely different from their own lives. Books and stories that contain moral dilemmas are often a favorite of secondary students. I believe this is because these stories allow students to think critically about life choices in an imagined world and possibly help them to prepare for some of their own future experiences.

Sequential Lessons for Transforming

Lesson 1 (Teacher-Directed): Introducing the Power

The focus of this lesson is modeling how books have the power to change the way we think about ourselves and the world.

In this lesson, students are introduced to the terms *transform* and *synthesize*.

- Ask students if they know what the word *transform* means. Give students a chance to suggest answers. Hopefully you can lead them to the idea that to transform means to change. Ask students for examples of things they know that transform (caterpillar into butterfly; transformer toy from robot to vehicle; tadpole into frog).
- Ask students if they know what the word *synthesize* means. By high school, most students have learned the word in a scientific context, usually in chemistry. In a synthesis reaction in chemistry, two elements combine to form a new product. They might have also heard of a synthesizer in music (different musical sounds combined to create a new sound) or synthetic fabric (different fibres combined to create a new material). In language arts, some of them might have encountered the dreaded synthesis essay, in which they discuss two pieces of literature. To synthesize means to combine two or more things into something new.
- Tell students that sometimes our thinking about ourselves and the world can change, based on something that we read. We combine the thoughts we already have in our brain with something from the text to create new thinking.
- If you have a special story that you keep returning to, share that with students and explain why it has had such an impact on you. Think back to life-lesson books that really influenced the way you think about the world.

  My life-lesson story is "Love You Forever" by Robert Munsch. I cannot get through this book without tearing up because it makes me think of my aging parents. I first encountered this book at a time in my life when I was really starting to notice just how much older my parents were becoming. This book made me realize that I need to make an effort to spend more time with my parents.

- Ask students to think back to books or stories that have stuck in their minds over the years. Allow students time to share out their favorites; ask students who share why the story is so important to them.

  Stories stick with us because we are able to take the author's words and combine them with our own thoughts and experiences to create new thinking.

- End the lesson by telling students that, over the next few lessons, they will be practicing finding transformations in various texts.

Lesson 2 (Guided Practice): Interacting with the Power

This lesson focuses on developing an Important Message statement for a story.

In this lesson, students are introduced to the idea of the author's purpose for writing a story.

- Discuss with students the idea that, because transforming requires the addition of our own thoughts, some stories will cause different transformations for different people. In the same way that different readers make different connections to text, not every story will cause a true transformation for every reader. However, we can usually understand what message the author was intending to communicate with their words. Explain that a message is usually something the author wants the reader to learn or take away from the story but that often is not written explicitly.

Recommended texts: "The Curio Shop" by William Kotzwinkle or *Mr. Peabody's Apples* by Madonna; Aesop's Fables are also excellent for this lesson.

- Select a grade-level story with a strong message or theme to read with students.
- Tell students that, while you are reading, they will be acting like news reporters, trying to decide what the author's important message is. From this message, they will work together to form a news headline for the story. They need to consider the following: Why did the author decide to tell this particular story? What was the author hoping to communicate to the reader? What life lessons can we learn from this story?
- Read the story with students, pausing during reading to draw students' attention to important events, and to model your connections, visualizations, questions, and inferences.
- When you finish reading the story, have students share with a partner what they think the message is.
- Once students have had time to share with a partner, have a whole-class discussion about the message. Brainstorm a list of things that the class learned from the story. See if the majority of students can agree on one lesson that is really important to be the class's Important Message for the story.
- Once students have agreed on one message, work as a class to develop an Important Message news flash, including a headline, about the story. For example:

   Don't Lie or People Won't Believe You When It Counts
   A young shepherd boy constantly tricked his neighbors into coming to the rescue of his sheep from fake wolf attacks. When the wolf really did attack, the boy's cries fell on deaf ears as his neighbors ignored his pleas. The wolf killed the young boy's entire flock of sheep. Let this be a lesson to all you fibbers out there. If you tell too many lies, eventually people won't believe anything you say.

Lesson 3 (Guided Practice): Interacting with the Power

The focus of this lesson is helping students identify specific opportunities for transformation through literature.

See page 72 for Issue/Theme chart.

In this lesson, students practice identifying issues presented in popular fairy tales and creating thematic statements from these issues.

- For this lesson, create a chart with the headings *Story*, *Issue*, and *Thematic Statement*.
- Under *Story*, list three fairy tales that most students will be familiar with: e.g., The Three Little Pigs, Little Red Riding Hood, Cinderella.
- For the first fairy tale, list in the appropriate column the issue presented in the story and a thematic statement that is connected to the issue. The thematic statement should be the thing that the reader could learn from the fairy tale and how the author communicated the message. See sample on page 66.
- For the second fairy tale, list the issue presented and a thematic statement; however, don't include how the thematic statement is communicated. See sample on page 66.
- For the third fairy tale, include just the issue presented and leave the column for the thematic statement blank. See sample on page 66.
- Leave the last two rows blank for students to fill in.
- Hand out the chart to students. Discuss the first example, for which you have provided all of the information. Direct students' attention to the fact that the

thematic statement is connected to the issue and has an explanation about how the author communicates the message.

- Discuss the second example. Again, direct students' attention to the fact that the thematic statement is connected to the issue identified in the second column. As a class, work to explain how the thematic statement is communicated to the reader through the story.
- Discuss the third example. For this one, only the issue has been identified. Work as a class to create a thematic statement and to explain how the author communicates the thematic statement to the reader.
- Divide students into partners. With their partner, students need to add two of their own examples to the chart. Remind them that their thematic statements need to be connected to the identified issue and that they need to explain how the author communicates the thematic statement to the reader.
- After students have had some time to add to their charts, have a few students share out with the class. Make sure that they have connected their thematic statement to the issue and that they have identified how the author communicates the thematic statement to the reader.
- Collect charts as formative assessment.

SAMPLE ISSUE/THEME CHART

Story	Issue	Thematic Statement
The Three Little Pigs	*Hard Work*	*Hard work pays off because the third pig works hard and his house stands up* *or* *Hard work doesn't pay off because all the pigs survive because of one pig's effort.*
Cinderella	*Kindness*	*Kindness will be rewarded because…*
Little Red Riding Hood	*Trust*	

Lesson 4 (Guided Practice): Interacting With the Power

In this lesson, students write a letter to themselves from the author about the special message contained in the story.

- Select a grade-level text with a strong theme or message.
- Select one word that describes the theme or meaning of the story. For example, love, trust, loss, and friendship are common themes in young adult literature. The word you choose must be connected to the story that you select.
- Write the word on the board. Tell students that you are going to read them a story connected to the word.
- Ask students to take out a piece of paper, write the word at the top, and record any thoughts or connections that they currently have for that word. Once they have finished, invite students to share their ideas with a partner.
- Tell students that, while you read, they need to try to find out what this book can teach them about that word. Tell them to pretend that the author has written a special message into the story just for them. Many will probably have

The focus of this lesson is to practice changing thinking based on reading. This lesson is adapted from a lesson found in *Reading Power* (2015) by Adrienne Gear.

Recommended texts: "Harrison Bergeron" by Kurt Vonnegut (diversity) or "The Gift of the Magi" by O. Henry (selflessness).

similar messages, but each of the messages will have a slightly different connection to each reader. Tell them that while you read, they should be paying special attention to how the word is connected to the story. Invite them to record their thoughts about the special word while you read.

- Read the story with students, pausing to model your own thinking and to allow them time to write down their thinking.
- When you finish reading the story, allow students time to record new additions to their thinking based on the story. Remind them that they must support their thinking with direct references to the text. Model your own changes in thinking for students.
- Finally, on the back of their paper, each student will write a letter to themselves from the author. In this letter, they will tell themselves what the special message in the story is, and how this message connects to both the text and the reader.
- End the lesson with a discussion about how the text could cause the reader's thinking to change based on the message. Collect recorded thinking and letters for formative assessment.

Lesson 5 (Guided Practice): Interacting With the Power

In this lesson, students practice identifying the plot and theme of a story.

The focus of this lesson is helping students differentiate between what happens in a story and what the theme of the story is.

See page 73 for the Plot/Message chart.

- With the class, review the meaning of *transformation* or *synthesis*.
- Tell students that you want to make sure that they know the difference between the plot of a story and the meaning or message of the story.
- Provide students with a two-column chart with *Plot* written on the left, and *Message/Theme* written on the right.
- Tell them that while you are reading, you want them to record the events of the story in the *Plot* column and any important lessons or learning in the *Message/Theme* column. This is a concrete way of helping students see the difference between plot and meaning.

Picture books are a great option for this lesson because they are short enough to read multiple times during the lesson and they usually contain strong themes. Recommended picture books: *The Girl Who Never Made Mistakes* by Mark Pett; *The Great Kapok Tree* by Lynne Cherry.

- Read the story with students, pausing to allow students time to record their thoughts on the chart. At the end of the story, come together as a class for a share out.
- End the lesson with a discussion of how the text could change the reader's thinking about the topic presented in the message. Collect the charts for formative assessment.

SAMPLE PLOT/MESSAGE CHART: *THE GREAT KAPOK TREE* **BY LYNNE CHERRY**

If you aren't able to find a picture book in your library, try searching the title on YouTube. *The Great Kapok Tree* is a book you will find as a video read-aloud, complete with sound effects from the Amazon Rainforest.

Plot	Message/Theme
A young man tries to chop down a huge kapok tree in the Amazon Rainforest. While he is sleeping, animals whisper to him the importance of the tree.	• wildlife preservation • interconnectedness of nature • environmental awareness

Plot	Message/Theme
A shopowner tries to sell a useless globe with an interesting history.	Our Earth is valuable and must be taken care of.

Lesson 6 (Guided Practice): Interacting with the Power

This lesson focuses on the difference between what happens in a story (the plot) and the meaning of the story (the theme).

In this lesson, students match previously read stories with the plots and themes for each story.

- For this lesson, you will revisit some of the stories that you have already used in the class. Before the lesson, make a list of stories you have read in the class on one sheet of paper.
- On a separate piece of paper, make a list of the plots for each of these stories. Try to limit plots to three to five sentences each.
- On a third piece of paper, make a list of the themes or messages that go with each of the stories on your list.
- Print out copies of all lists. Cut lists into strips with one story, plot, or list of themes each, and put the strips into envelopes. Make sure to have one envelope for every two or three students. Every envelope should have the story titles, plots, and themes in it.
- On the day of the lesson, hand out envelopes to groups of students and have them sort the strips into story title, plot, and theme. Grouping students allows those who might have missed one or two stories to participate in the lesson.
- Once students have completed their sort, have them check with one other group to make sure that they all agree on the sort. Once they have double-checked, have students glue the sorted strips onto a piece of paper.
- Collect the sorted strips for formative assessment.

Lesson 7 (Independent Practice): Using the Power

This lesson focuses on the difference between the plot and the theme of a text.

In this lesson, students write a two-paragraph response summarizing the plot and the theme of a text.

- Find a grade-level text to read with students.
- With the class, review the difference between the plot and the theme or message. Tell students that, while you are reading the story, they need to be making notes about both the plot and the message of the text.
- Read the story with students. You can provide them with a blank copy of the Plot/Message chart on page 73 to record their thoughts. Some students prefer to make their own notes as they read.
- When you finish the story, have students write a two-paragraph response to the story, summarizing both the plot and the message of the story. If they use the chart, the first column will form their plot paragraph and the second column will form their message or theme paragraph. Their second paragraph should also include information about how the story could cause the reader to think differently about the topic presented in the theme.
- Collect paragraphs for formative assessment.

Transformed Thinking	NYM	M	FM	EX
Understands that transformed thinking is s new way of thinking about a topic				
Is able to distinguish between the text and their thinking				
Can provide examples of how information from the text combined with background knowledge to create transformed thinking				
Is able to synthesize information from multiple sources with background knowledge				

Focus Literary Device: Theme

Theme is one of the most complex concepts for students to understand. The idea of transforming provides students with a different way of thinking about theme. It can be helpful to communicate to students that theme is the transformation that the author was hoping to cause for the reader. It is a new way of thinking, or a new way of looking at the world. The theme requires the addition of the reader's thoughts; it is the synthesis of the author's story and the reader's way of thinking. Theme is the reason that the author wrote the story; it's the answer to *So what?* for the piece of literature. While not every story will transform every reader, every story does have a message or theme that that author wants to communicate.

Events in the Text = Plot
Author's message + Reader's thoughts = Theme

Sample Lesson: Letter to the Author

Have students write a letter to the author of a story or book that has transformed their thinking. Students can pick from texts that you have read in class or from texts that they have read on their own.

- Start by having students identify where/when they read the text. For example:

  I first encountered The Fault in Our Stars *when a student recommended it to me. Once I started reading it, I couldn't stop.*

- Next, have students explain how the text affected them, or how it transformed their thinking. For example:

  Your book gave me new insight into how I believe we should live our lives. The truth is, life is messy and hard and sometimes it really sucks. However, we can't experience all of the good things if we try to avoid the challenging things.

Students could also e-mail the author or publisher and take a screenshot of their letter to hand in for assessment.

- Finally, students should thank the author for writing a text that influenced their lives.

Sample Lesson: Book Review

Have students write a review of the text. This could be done online with websites like amazon.ca or goodreads.com.

- In their review, students describe and explain how the text addresses the theme.
- Remind students that good reviews offer commentary but never reveals too much about important events or the ending of the text. For example:

    The Fault in Our Stars *lets the reader explore what it's like living with a potentially terminal illness. In this novel, the main character learns that the only thing worse than dying is not living life to the fullest. This novel is a great read for both teenagers and adults.*

- For assessment, students can hand in a copy of their review, or they could provide you with their screen name and the title of the book they reviewed so you can go online to read it.

Prompts and Sentence Frames to Encourage Transforming

- *The author communicates the theme of… by…*
- How has your thinking changed after reading the text?
- *I now understand that…*
- Describe several insights that you have gained from the text.
- *I used to think… but now I'm thinking…*
- What have you learned about life from the text?
- Discuss what the author is trying to tell the reader about life.
- Find a quote that demonstrates how you want to live your life. Describe what this quote illustrates.
- Why do you think the author wrote this text?
- Describe three events from the text that help communicate the theme or message.
- What moral or life lesson is illustrated by the story? How does the author communicate this?
- Describe one change that you will try to make in your life because of this story. Why?

Books listed are appropriate for use with high-school students. Those that could also be used in middle-school classes are marked with an M.

Suggested Texts for Transforming

Thirteen Reasons Why by Jay Asher (novel)

"A Poison Tree" by William Blake (poem, M)

The Great Kapok Tree by Lynne Cherry (picture book, M)

"The Taste of Melon" by Borden Deal (short story, M)

The Elephant Mountains by Scott Ely (novel)

"The Fifty-First Dragon" by Heywood Broun (short story)

"The Gift of the Magi" by O. Henry (short story)

"The Lottery" by Shirley Jackson (short story)

"The Possibility of Evil" by Shirley Jackson (short story)

"If" by Rudyard Kipling (poem, M)

"The Curio Shop" by William Kotzwinkle (short story, M)

Whimsy's Heavy Things by Julie Kraulis (picture book, M)

"The Rocking-Horse Winner" by D.H. Lawrence (short story)

Rules by Cynthia Lord (novel, M)

The Invisible Boy by Trudy Ludwig (picture book, M)

Mr. Peabody's Apples by Madonna (picture book, M)

1984 by George Orwell (novel)

"Dulce Et Decorum Est" by Wilfred Owen (poem)

The Girl Who Never Made Mistakes by Mark Pett (picture book, M)

Max the Mighty by Rodman Philbrick (novel, M)

Monkey Beach by Eden Robinson (novel; strong content)

"I Am Graffiti" by Leanne Simpson (poem)

Migrant by Maxine Trottier (picture book, M)

"Harrison Bergeron" by Kurt Vonnegut Jr. (short story)

"Returning to Harmony" by Richard Wagamese (personal essay)

Dot by Randi Zuckerberg (picture book, M)

Issue/Theme

Story	Issue	Thematic Statement

Pembroke Publishers © 2016 *Powerful Readers* by Kyla Hadden and Adrienne Gear ISBN 978-1-55138-313-2

Plot/Message

Plot	Message/Theme

PART B

Nonfiction Reading Power

Whether reading fiction or nonfiction, readers need access to the same decoding strategies. Comprehension when reading information, however, differs slightly from when reading stories. While readers can still make connections, ask questions, and infer, they are not making predictions or visualizing as often when reading nonfiction. They are, however, identifying key pieces of information and using text features and text prompts to help them access the information.

Just as fiction authors use literary techniques, such as imagery, metaphor, and flashback, to help readers comprehend, nonfiction authors use specific techniques to help their readers access information. Nonfiction text features are a way writers of nonfiction enhance readers' understanding. Using specific text structures that match the purpose of their writing is another way nonfiction writers support their readers' comprehension. Because nonfiction tends to focus more on communicating specific information than on entertainment, good readers need to be able to identify the important information from texts and summarize it.

The list of nonfiction reading powers has both similarities and differences from that of the fiction reading powers:

CONNECTING

Powerful readers make connections to experiences and background knowledge to enhance their understanding of nonfiction texts. They monitor where new information fits with their prior knowledge. They understand that their brain is better able to make sense of and store information when it is linked to prior knowledge.

ZOOMING-IN

Powerful readers are able to recognize, locate, and interpret nonfiction text features. They understand that authors use text features to direct the reader's attention to important information and to help communicate important ideas.

DETERMINING IMPORTANCE

Powerful readers are able to find the main ideas in nonfiction texts. To do this, they make use of their knowledge of both text features and structures. They also understand that readers use different strategies, depending on the structure of the text they are reading. Being able to identify text structures helps them guide their attention to important information. They understand that the reader's purpose for reading helps determine what information is important. They are able to set aside information that does not fit their purpose for reading.

QUESTIONING/INFERRING

Powerful readers ask questions and make inferences to further their understanding of nonfiction texts. They ask questions before they read to focus their thinking, while they read to check for understanding, and after they read to extend their understanding. They also understand that sometimes they need to infer meaning based on the text and their own knowledge.

TRANSFORMING (OR SYNTHESIZING)

Powerful readers are able to recognize a change in their own thinking, perception, or perspective that comes through reading a piece of nonfiction text. They can combine their old knowledge with the knowledge gained from a piece of text to create slightly new knowledge.

8 Connecting

"Students who have background knowledge about a topic have a real advantage because they can connect the new information they encounter to what they already know." (Harvey and Goudvis, 2007)

Most of us have had the experience of trying to read a piece of technical text on a topic we have little connection to or prior knowledge of—think about trying to read a university physics textbook on dark matter with little to no understanding of the basic laws of physics. It would be next to impossible! In our classrooms, we would never try to teach our students a concept they had no background knowledge about. The idea of connecting new knowledge to prior knowledge to improve learning is nothing new. Those K–W–L (Know–Wonder–Learn) charts we were taught to use in teacher training weren't just a fun suggestion to amuse our students. They actually help prep our brains for learning, set a purpose, and allow us to reflect on how our knowledge has changed after we have gathered new information.

Students also need practice making connections between their own experiences and the texts they are reading. Often they treat each individual text like a completely separate source of information; however, in-depth study of a topic requires the reader to notice how the information from different sources fits together and connects to what they already know about the topic. I quite often use the symbol of an anchor when talking about connecting: our connections act like an anchor that holds new information in place.

I like to teach the nonfiction connecting lessons following the fiction connecting lessons, as nonfiction connecting can be more difficult. Students usually find it easier to connect things to their own experiences than to make connections between new knowledge and old knowledge. Keep in mind that it is never recommended that you teach reading skills in isolation. Learning how to improve reading skills is best done during the process of reading something meaningful. There is no point in learning literacy skills if they are not connected to an actual purpose. Readers and writers need something meaningful to read and write about.

Like fiction connections, there are three types of nonfiction connections:
Text-to-Self: personal experiences
Text-to-Text: books, movies, TV, etc.
Text-to-World: something we know from the world

This series of connecting lessons is designed around a specific unit. If I am teaching a content-area class, I select a short unit of study that would normally take around two weeks to complete as my connecting *anchor*. If I am teaching an English course, I usually select a short unit around a current event. The topic needs to be manageable enough that you can explore it in a short amount of time; for example, WWI is too big a topic, but trench warfare would be just right. Each sequential lesson builds on the learning from the previous lesson. At the beginning of each lesson, students reflect on their prior knowledge about the topic. These lessons are designed to be integrated with some of the activities that you would already do as part of the unit of study. Don't throw out the good things you are already doing!

Sequential Lessons for Connecting

Lesson 1 (Teacher-Directed): Introducing the Power

In this lesson, the teacher introduces students to the idea of connecting new knowledge to prior knowledge.

The focus of this lesson is to model connecting for students.

- If you have already done fiction connecting lessons with your students—and this is recommended—remind them of how connections help us understand more about the text.
- Tell students to think of their brains as having three *pockets* (see margin note on page 30) where they store information: one for memories, one for facts, one for imagination.
- Continue the lesson:

> *The pocket you access for connections will depend on your purpose for reading. When reading nonfiction, we tend to rely more on the facts that we know. Although our memories of personal experiences can help us when reading nonfiction, they don't always help us make sense of fact-based information. We don't often dip into our imagination brain pocket when reading nonfiction, because we want to honor the genre of nonfiction, which means that we need to stay with the truth and information from the real world.*

I ask students to suggest a fact-based topic for this lesson. Usually they try to trip me up with a really complex topic, like brain surgery or rocket science. If you are not brave enough to put yourself at the whim of your students' suggestions, have a topic already selected.

- Tell students you are going to model how good readers approach nonfiction pieces.
- Write a topic on the board. Under the topic, create columns with the headings *Things I Know for Sure* and *Things I Think I Know*. Discuss and model the concept that sometimes we think we know things but may not be 100% sure.

If you are involved in content-area study of a specific topic, you could use this lesson to explore students' background knowledge about the topic. Start by providing students with a few of your own examples, and then have the class fill in the rest of the chart. I tell students that I can put something in the *Things I Know for Sure* chart only if no one disagrees with the point. That way we honor all students' input without reinforcing any misconceptions.

- Under each column make a list of your own prior knowledge about the topic. Remind students that most of this connecting usually occurs in the reader's head but, because thinking is invisible, you are writing it down for them to see. For example, if my topic was World War I, I might write *took place in Europe* in the first column and *involved Germany* in the second column.
- Tell students that over the next few lessons they will be learning about making connections between new knowledge and prior knowledge, and between multiple information sources.

Lesson 2 (Guided Practice): Interacting with the Power

In this lesson, students record their prior knowledge about the topic they are about to study.

The focus of this lesson is the concept that each reader brings slightly different connections to a piece of nonfiction text.

- Tell students the topic you will be exploring for the next few lessons (i.e., the topic that fits your context or is linked to a subject the students are exploring in a content-area class).

See page 82 for the Know/Think I Know chart.

- Hand out copies of the Know/Think I Know chart on page 82. Tell students you are going to start by giving them two minutes to record the things that they know or think they know about the topic.
- Have students share their responses with a partner. If the partner suggests something that they know but forgot to write down, they can record it on their chart.

- Have students select a new partner and share. Again, if their partner suggests something that they know but forgot to write down, they can record it on their chart.
- End the lesson by having students discuss one thing in their *Think I Know* column with a partner. Challenge them to turn that point into a question to be researched later. Collect charts for formative assessment.

Lesson 3 (Guided Practice): Interacting with the Power

The focus of this lesson is making connections between different texts and activating prior knowledge through photographs.

In this lesson, students practice making connections between a series of photographs.

- Choose a series of three photographs centred on the topic from the preceding lesson. You will need a way of projecting the photographs in a format large enough for students to pick out details from their seats.
- Divide students into pairs. Each partnership must decide who is partner *A* and who is partner *B*.
- Tell students you are going to show them a short series of photographs. Their job is to describe each photograph to their partner, and to look for things they can learn about the topic of study.

See page 83 for the Connecting with Photographs chart.

- Hand out the Connecting with Photographs chart on page 83. Have students record the prior knowledge that they wrote about in the preceding lesson. Tell them that this information will help activate their brains for today's new knowledge. If students can't remember what they wrote down, hand out the Know/Think I Know charts from the previous lesson.
- Have students position themselves so that partner *A* can see the photograph, but partner *B* cannot. Partner *A* will have two minutes to describe the photograph to their partner. Both partners will record the description on their chart. Tell *A* partners that their description needs to be detailed enough that their partner has enough information to complete their chart.
- Project the first photograph for students to see. Give them two minutes to describe the photo and one minute to record their information on the charts. Once the time is up, remove the first photograph from the screen.
- Have students switch places so that partner *B* can see the photograph and partner *A* cannot. This time partner *B* will have two minutes to describe the photograph to their partner. Again, both partners must record the description on their charts.
- Project the second photograph for students to see. Give two minutes to describe the photo and one minute to record their information on their charts. Once the time is up, remove the second photograph.
- Have students move so that both partners can see the photographs as you project them.
- Tell students that you are going to show them a third photograph. This time both partners will be able to see it. Instead of one partner describing the photo, partners will discuss it and then record their information on their charts.
- Project the third photograph. Give students two minutes to discuss the photograph and one minute to record their information on the charts.
- Show all three photographs to students again, one at a time. Give them a moment to discuss how accurate their partner's description was. Tell them that now their job is to look for connections between the photographs. They can continue to work in partners to record any connections on their charts.

- Once students have had a few minutes to work with their partners on connections, have students share with the class any connections that they found. Tell students that if someone shares a connection that they agree with, they can record that connection on their chart.
- End the lesson by discussing how we can "read" photographs and get information from them. Discuss why it was important to look for connections between the three photographs. Draw students' attention to the idea that, when we are learning about a topic, we need to think about how the different sources fit together. Collect charts for formative assessment.

Lesson 4 (Guided Practice): Interacting with the Power

In this lesson, students practice making connections between two different written texts.

The focus of this lesson is building on prior knowledge and connections between nonfiction texts.

- For this lesson, you will need to select two short nonfiction articles on your topic of study. You will need one copy of each article per pair of students.
- Tell students that in this lesson, they are going to compare the information presented in two different sources.
- Hand out the Connecting with Texts chart on page 84.

See page 84 for the Connecting with Texts chart.

- Partner up students. Hand out one copy of each article to each pair. Have them decide which partner is going to read which article. Tell students that they need to read their article and record the main points from it in the left column. Give students a few minutes to read the article and record the main points.
- Once students have read their own article and recorded the main points, they need to explain their article to their partner. Each partner needs to fill in the second column of the chart based on their partner's information.
- Tell students that, with their partner, they need to look for connections between the two articles. Did they contain any similar information? Did they contain any contradictory information? Have students record their connections on the chart.
- Once students have had a few minutes to work with partners to discuss and record connections, have them share out with the class any connections that they noticed. Students can add new connections to their charts if they agree with them.

Writing Connection: Have students write a compare-and-contrast paragraph about two articles on the same topic. Have them look for areas where the articles agreed about information and areas where they contained different ideas.

- End the lesson by asking students to reflect on this experience. How did their understanding differ when they read the article themselves compared to when their partner explained their article to them? How did making connections between the two articles enhance their understanding? Collect charts for formative assessment.

Lesson 5 (Independent Practice): Using the Power

In this lesson, students practice making connections between an article and information found on a webpage.

The focus of this lesson is applying the skill of making connections to nonfiction text.

- For this lesson, provide students with an article on your selected topic. Students will also need access to the Internet.
- Tell students that they will be applying what they have learned about connecting to make connections between an article provided by the teacher and a website on the Internet.
- Hand out the Connecting with Texts from Different Sources chart on page 85. Give them a few minutes to record their prior knowledge on the topic. The

See page 85 for the Connecting with Texts from Different Sources chart.

information in this section should be increasing as students interact with a variety of sources on the topic of study.

- Tell students they need to read the article that you have provided and record the main points from the article on the Connecting chart.
- Once students have finished with the article, they need to find a reliable website on that same topic. Tell students that they might not need the whole website; they may need to read only the section that is on the topic you are studying. Have students record important information from the website on the Connecting with Texts from Different Sources chart.
- Once students have had a chance to read and record information from their website, they need to focus on finding connections between the two sources. Do the sources support each other? Do they contain some similar information?
- End the lesson by reflecting on the process: How did their articles compare? Which source did they find easier to read? Which was more informative? Why would it be important to read more than one source when researching a topic? Collect charts for summative assessment.

ASSESSMENT RUBRIC FOR CONNECTING

Making Connections	NYM	M	FM	EX
Is able to make connections to background knowledge and experiences				
Recognizes the difference between text-to-self, text-to-text, and text-to-world connections				
Is able to make connections between multiple texts				
Can explain how a connection extends thinking				

Curricular Connections for Connecting

All Subjects: Using Multiple Sources

The ability to make text-to-text connections is an important skill for older students to develop. Text-to-text connections form the basis of synthesizing information from multiple sources. Take a moment to think back to research that you completed as part of your undergraduate or graduate work; most of it likely involved connecting information from multiple sources. Successful researchers are able to make connections between texts. In order to scaffold this for students, it is important to start small. Create learning opportunities for students to make connections between two or three texts

All Subjects: Evaluating Sources

Students are often unsure what to do when two sources contain conflicting information. If I had a dollar for every time a student came to me saying, "This website says this date, but this other website says this date," I'd be a rich woman! The Connecting lessons are a great way to start a conversation around evaluating sources. We sometimes think that, because our students are tech savvy, they know how to navigate the different sources of information found online. This is not the case! Our students need tools to help them determine the reliability of websites. There are many different tools for evaluating sources; your school may already have something in place that the students are familiar with.

One of my favorites is the C.R.A.P. (yes, the kids eat this one up) system developed by Mercer University in the Unites States. C.R.A.P. stands for Currency, Relevancy, Authority, and Purpose. Students work through a series of questions about when the source was produced, does it inform the topic, who wrote it, and why did they write it.

Sentence Frames to Support Nonfiction Connections

- *My connection is _____. This helps me understand (the text) because…*
- *I knew about _____ (something from my brain) and it helped me understand _____(something from the text) because _____.*
- *Now I think _____ because in the text it said _____.*
- *One source told me _____ and another source told me _____. That makes me think that _____.*
- *Both sources had information on _____. That makes me understand that _____.*

Know/Think I Know

Topic:	
Things I know about this topic	Things I think I know about this topic

Connecting with Photographs

Prior knowledge about this topic:

Photograph 1	Photograph 2	Photograph 3
Description:	Description:	Description:
New Knowledge:	New Knowledge:	New Knowledge:

Connections between the three photographs:

Pembroke Publishers © 2016 *Powerful Readers* by Kyla Hadden and Adrienne Gear ISBN 978-1-55138-313-2

Connecting with Texts

Prior knowledge about this topic:

Article Title:	Article Title:
Main Points:	Main Points:

Connections between the two articles:

Pembroke Publishers © 2016 *Powerful Readers* by Kyla Hadden and Adrienne Gear ISBN 978-1-55138-313-2

Connecting with Texts from Different Sources

Prior knowledge about this topic:

Article Title:	Website URL/Title:
Main Points:	Main Points:

Connections between the two sources:

Pembroke Publishers © 2016 *Powerful Readers* by Kyla Hadden and Adrienne Gear ISBN 978-1-55138-313-2

9 Zooming In

"Information is found in many places on the page of nonfiction text, and is presented in a variety of ways: on a graph or in a chart, highlighted in a fact box, or featured as a caption under a photograph." (Gear, 2008)

While I was marking a secondary reading assessment with a colleague, we made a startling discovery in the vocabulary section. Even though the reading passage contained a glossary on each page, many students could not define a word defined on that page. They were skipping over some of the text features and focusing on the main body of the passage.

Content-area teachers have probably had similar experiences with students who could not locate information if it was located outside the main body of the text. Before I explicitly taught text features to my students, many were unable to find the answers to questions when the answer was located in a text feature. Many students see charts, glossaries, and pictures as "extras," containing less-valuable information than the main body of the text. Some may be familiar with the terms *glossary*, *chart*, and *map*, but being able to identify features is not enough. Students must learn how to locate and access information from them.

The power of Zooming In really means the ability to understand the role of text features in comprehension. Text features, such as maps, pictures, diagrams, and headings, are basically clues and tools the author has provided to help the reader locate and access information. If the author wants to clearly communicate to readers the different parts of a machine, he/she provides an illustration of the machine with labels identifying the parts. While this information could be communicated using only words, the use of a diagram helps some, if not all, readers more readily comprehend the information. Text features help readers navigate through the complexity of the text, often organizing and highlighting key information.

Unlike fiction, where the majority of information is communicated through words in the main body of text, nonfiction uses a variety of forms to help the reader access the information. These text features serve two purposes: to help organize information and to provide information. Headings, tables of contents, and special fonts all help the reader locate information, directing readers' attention to important ideas. Some text features, such as pictures, diagrams, charts, and graphs, provide a visual representation of information to help the reader access information more easily and comprehend important ideas. They are there to enhance the readers' experience with the text.

The ability to navigate text features can be connected directly to determining importance, as text features are one of the clues readers use to help them separate important information from unimportant information. Headings give the reader clues about the purpose of a certain section. Special fonts draw the reader's attention to important words or ideas. Glossaries provide the reader with definitions for important words or concepts. Quite often, the author will repeat important information found in the main body of a text within or alongside a text feature designed to enhance the reader's understanding of that idea. In short, text features are a reader's best friend and should not be ignored.

Sequential Lessons for Zooming-In

Lesson 1 (Teacher-Directed): Introducing the Power

The focus of this lesson is developing an awareness of the different tools authors use to organize information for the reader.

In this lesson, students compare two pieces of text: one without text features and one with text features.

- Choose a short article or textbook extract that relates to the subject you are studying. Make sure that it uses multiple text features.
- Rewrite the information in the text, removing all the text features. There should be nothing on the page except for information written in paragraph form. Another option for this lesson is to search the Internet for short pieces on the same topic. One of the pieces should have a lot of text features, the other should be organized mainly by paragraphs with few organizational text features. Make copies of the two texts: half the students will have the text-feature–rich copy, and half the students will have the rewritten piece.
- Randomly pass out the two different versions of the text so that half the class has the text-feature–rich passage and the others have the text-only version. Instruct them to read the passage and record the important information.
- Have students partner with someone who has the other version of the text. Have them compare the two texts as well as the information they pulled out of the text. If time allows, have students create a Venn diagram for the two texts. Did the two pieces have any important information in common? Did they share any text features, such as titles or headings? If you like, this Venn diagram can be collected for formative assessment.
- Ask students to decide with their partner which text was easier to read and gather information from. Although a few students may prefer the mostly-text piece, as a rule, most people prefer nonfiction pieces that use text features. Explain that this may have something to do with our brains being able to process only so much text on one page.
- As a class, discuss which piece students like better. Brainstorm a list of things they liked about each piece. Ask students which one was easier to read; which one their brains liked more.
- Finally, as a class, brainstorm a list of text features used in the articles. Check the sample list on page 88.

Lesson 2 (Guided Practice): Interacting with the Power

The focus of this lesson is identifying common text features and the information communicated by each feature.

In this lesson students search for examples of text features.

- Hand out a list of the common nonfiction text features. Depending on the age and level of your students, you may want to use only some of the text features. Many of these might be ones that students came up with at the conclusion of the preceding lesson.

SAMPLE LIST OF TEXT FEATURES

Web	Caption	Venn Diagram	Chart
Table of Contents	Map	Fact Box	Sidebar
Label	Comparison	Index	Photograph
Heading	Special Font	Diagram	Glossary
Picture	Title	Flow Chart	Close-Up or Inset

To incorporate technology into the lesson, have students do a digital scavenger hunt. Students can go to the library or bring their own textbooks to class and take pictures of examples of each of the text features they find. They can then compile the pictures into a Word document or PowerPoint file.

- Divide students into pairs or small groups. Hand out the Text Features chart on page 92. Have students search through a textbook (or any nonfiction book) to find examples of each feature on the list. Students need to list the page number that the text feature is found on and describe the information that was communicated by the text feature.
- End the lesson by asking students to reflect on the activity: What did you notice about text features during your search? Were some more commonly used than others? Why do you think some features are used more often than others? Collect the chart or scavenger-hunt results for formative assessment; students will be using it again for Lesson 4 on page 89.

Lesson 3 (Guided Practice): Interacting with the Power

In this lesson, students compare the information gathered from the main body of a text to that gathered from the text features of a text.

The focus of this lesson is noticing how much information is provided by the text features.

- Select a short grade-level nonfiction text that is rich in text features. Remove most of the text features before you give the text to students.
- Tell students that you want them to record the important information from a piece of text. Ask them to take out a piece of paper to record their information.
- Introduce students to the text you are working with. Look at the title and have them spend a few moments recording any prior knowledge they have on the subject area.
- Tell students that they will be working in partners to read through the text and pick out the important information about the topic.
- Provide students with time to read and take notes.
- Have students share out their important ideas with the class. This will give students in need of more scaffolding a chance to gather information from their classmates.
- Tell students that you gave them only part of the text. Hand out copies of the text in its original form with the text features. Ask students if they thought they missed out on any information by not having the text features.
- Tell students that you want to see just how much information they missed in the first reading. Tell students to make some additional notes about any important information located in the text features.
- Provide students with time to read and take notes.

This lesson will give you an idea of your students' abilities to determine importance. If your students struggle to gather the important details, you know that they will need a lot of practice with the reading power of Determining Importance (see chapter 10).

- Have students share out their important ideas from the text features with the class. Try to focus students' attention on how much information is often located in the text features.
- End the lesson by having students reflect on what they noticed about reading with and without text features. Collect students' notes for formative assessment.

Lesson 4 (Guided Practice): Interacting with the Power

The focus of this lesson is the idea that authors use some text features to organize information, and other text features to help draw the reader's attention to important information.

In this lesson, students will explore organizational versus informational text features.

- Tell students that some text features help the reader organize information and some actually contain information.
- Have students create a two-column chart on a blank piece of paper and write the heading *Organizational Features* at the top of one column and *Informational Features* at the top of the other.
- Hand back the chart or scavenger hunt that students completed for Lesson 2 (page 87). Tell them they need to decide which heading (*Organizational* or *Informational*) each text feature belongs under, based on their purpose. Students will write the name of the text feature under the correct heading.
- For organizational features, students will write what kind of direction the feature provides to the reader; for example, headings don't actually contain a lot of information but they do give the reader a clue about what information will be located in that section.
- For informational features, students will write what kind of information would fit under each feature; for example, maps are used to show location.
- End the lesson by asking students to reflect on the purposes for different kinds of features: When would a writer need to use informational features? Why would a writer choose a feature over writing a paragraph? Which is easier to write? Which is easier to read? Collect the chart for formative assessment.

Lesson 5 (Independent Practice): Using the Power

This lesson focuses on how text features can enhance the reader's understanding of a text.

See page 93 for the Text Feature/ Purpose list.

In this lesson, students apply what they have learned by reorganizing an article using organizational and informational text features.

- Select a grade-level nonfiction article that is lacking text features. You could use the one from the first lesson.
- Hand out the Text Feature/Purpose list on page 93. As a class, review the purpose for each text feature. If you can, refer back to previous lessons to come up with examples for each one.
- Tell students they need to carefully read the information, and then reorganize and rewrite the article using text features, while preserving the information contained in the article. The goal is to enhance the text by adding both organizational and informational text features. They can cut up the article and reorganize it before gluing it onto a new sheet; they can add headings to each paragraph; they can add a glossary to define important words; they can use a highlighter to draw the reader's attention to important information.

Seymore Simon has written more 300 nonfiction books for children, none of which include text features. His books are filled with pages and pages of detailed information; however, because they lack text features, reading them can be challenging. They make good examples of how-not-to-write nonfiction texts!

- As an alternative, students can use the existing article as their research base and create their own one-page information page, using the existing information and enhancing it with text features.
- End the lesson by reflecting on the activity: How did making your own text features help you better understand the information you read? Do you think information is easier to access when it's in a feature or a paragraph? Why? Collect reorganized articles for summative assessment.

Using Text Features	NYM	M	FM	EX
Can identify and locate text features				
Recognizes the purpose of text features				
Understands the difference between organizational and information text features				
Uses text features to enhance understanding of text				

Curricular Connections for Zooming-In

Math: Text Features

Depending on the topic of study and the text features students are learning about, there are plenty of opportunities for you to integrate math skills into this unit.

GRAPHING

Teach students about the different kinds of graphs found in nonfiction texts. They need to know how to read them and how to create them.

COMPARISON

Studying comparisons provides a great opportunity for students to learn about scale and ratios. Note: if you provide readers with a comparison to enhance understanding of your information, you should know the math behind creating an accurate comparison.

All Subjects: Using Text Features

Microsoft Word or Publisher are usually used for these projects.

Once students can successfully use a strategy, you know they have mastered it. In both English and content-area classes, I always have students complete at least one written project for which they are required to use text features. I allow them to pick the topic; sometimes it's connected to something we are studying, sometimes it's the student's choice. There are two main requirements for the project: students must use at least five different text features; and the project must fit on one page. I use this project as a chance to teach students how to use text boxes or how to add captions to pictures and images. They also need to complete a reflection that explains how the text features they used could help the reader better understand their topic.

Sentence Frames to Support Zooming In

- *I like how the author used _____(insert text feature) to help me understand _____.*
- *How does the author use _____ (insert text feature) to help the reader?*
- *I wish the author would have used _____ (insert text feature) to help me understand _____.*
- *The _____(insert text feature) really helped me understand _____.*
- *I would use _____ (insert text feature) to help the reader understand _____.*

Text Features

Book title:		
Text Feature	Page Number	Describe the information communicated by the text feature
Heading		
Picture or Photograph		
Caption		
Table of Contents		
Index		
Glossary		
Special Font		
Chart		
Diagram		
Map		
Fact Box		
Sidebar		
Venn Diagram		
Label		
Comparison		
Title		
Web		
Flow Chart		
Close-Up or Inset		

Pembroke Publishers © 2016 *Powerful Readers* by Kyla Hadden and Adrienne Gear ISBN 978-1-55138-313-2

Text Feature/Purpose

Text Feature	Purpose
Organizational	
Special Fonts	Direct the reader's attention to important information
Label	One or two words that help the reader name an object or identify the parts of an object
Table of Contents	Shows the reader the different topics or sections in the book and the corresponding page numbers
Index	An alphabetical list of topics with page numbers to help the reader locate information
Heading	To help the reader locate specific information by naming the topic covered in the next part of the text
Glossary	To help the reader learn the meaning of words included in the text
Informational	
Venn Diagram	Shows similarities and differences between two or more topics
Captions	Tell the reader more about a picture or illustration
Charts or Tables	Show the reader qualities or comparisons between two or more sets of data
Pictures or Photographs	Show the reader exactly what something looks like
Map	To help the reader understand a graphical representation of a location. Maps often include symbols and a key.
Timeline	To help the reader by showing change or events over time. Timelines often include specific dates.
Cutaway	To help the reader understand something by looking at its form from the inside
Web	Shows elements related to a central theme or idea
Diagram	Illustration of something that can't be photographed. Diagrams often have labels.
Comparison	To help the reader understand one thing by comparing it to something else
Sidebar	To draw the reader's attention to interesting or important information. Definitions are often found in sidebars.
Fact Box	To draw the reader's attention to interesting or important information
Flow Chart	To illustrate the steps or connections between ideas, events, or people
Close-Up or Inset	Helps show small details; usually shows a focus on one part of a larger image.

Pembroke Publishers © 2016 *Powerful Readers* by Kyla Hadden and Adrienne Gear ISBN 978-1-55138-313-2

10 Determining Importance

"The main idea often depends on who the main reader is!" (Harvey and Goudvis, 2007)

Early in my career, I spent far too much time giving students information when I should have been teaching them how to uncover it for themselves. I was worried that students wouldn't be able to identify the information that I wanted them to focus on. Rather than teaching students how to determine importance and setting a purpose for reading, I gave them sets of notes that contained the information I wanted them to have. While it's true that this route may have been the fastest one, students quite often didn't remember the information I gave them because they hadn't actively interacted with it. If we want our students to become active consumers of information instead of passive recipients, we need to teach them to recognize important information.

In order to select important information, students need to know their purpose for reading a piece of text. Are they trying to answer a specific question, or are they just looking for interesting facts? I confess that, in the past, the only purpose I have given students for reading a piece of nonfiction text is to answer the assigned questions at the end of the chapter. When students are out on their own, researching a specific topic, they are often at a loss for what information to include and what information to leave behind. Harvey and Goudvis (2007) discuss the importance of teaching students to distinguish between what they think is the most important information and what the author thinks is the most important information. Powerful readers are able to distinguish between interesting facts they connect to and the main idea being presented by the author.

Powerful readers also know that their approach to reading information text needs to change depending on the structure of each text. Just as most fiction has predictable plot structures to help organize information about the story, nonfiction often follows specific structures depending on the type of information being presented. For example, problem–solution texts usually start by identifying the problem or question and end with an explanation or answer; sequence texts usually identify the topic and then list the steps or parts in a specific order. Imagine how much easier reading nonfiction text would be if the reader had an understanding of what order the information would be presented in! In addition, if the reader is aware of the text structure, there is a natural connection between the order of the text and important information. As with text features, text structure aids the reader in identifying where important information will be located.

Determining importance builds upon the reading powers you have already introduced to your students. For example, text features often provide the reader with clues that a reader might use to infer what information might be important in a piece of text. Or a reader might make a connection to a piece of information that is important to the meaning. It is important that we continue to model previously taught reading powers and provide students with opportunities to practice them.

Sequential Lessons for Determining Importance

Lesson 1 (Teacher-Directed): Introducing the Power

This lesson focuses on three steps for determining important information in a piece of nonfiction text.

In this lesson, the teacher models how to summarize a piece of nonfiction text.

- Select a short piece of text to read with students that is connected to something you are studying.
- Ask students how they decide what information is important when they read a piece of text.
- Tell students that you are going to model how to pick out important information. While you are modeling your thinking, students need to record the steps that you share.
- Project the text so that everyone can read it. Step 1: Mention that we need to have a specific purpose for reading; just what this purpose is depends on what we are reading. Share out your purpose for reading this passage.
- Step 2: See if you can figure out what the structure of the text is. Tell students that this helps you figure out what information the author was trying to communicate.
- Step 3: Model how you look at nonfiction text features to look for clues about what information is important.
- Tell students that, over the next lessons, they will be practicing how to determine importance in nonfiction texts.

Reproducible grade-level passages are often difficult to come by. Try Evan-Moore's series Nonfiction Reading Practice, which includes content-specific articles with passages at three different reading levels; Scholastic's *Hi-Lo Nonfiction Passages, Grades 6–8*, or Scholastic's *25 Complex Text Passages to Meet the Common Core: Literature and Informational Texts, Grade 7–8*.

Lesson 2 (Guided Practice): Interacting with the Power

The focus of this lesson is connecting importance to purpose.

In this lesson, students must choose from a list of items based on an assigned scenario.

- Tell students that they are packing for a two-week vacation. The only catch is, they have a very small suitcase that can only hold 15 items. Immediately, students will ask about their destination and the time of year. Tell them that the destination and timing of the vacation is secret. They won't know where they are going until they get there.
- Have students record their list on a piece of paper. Once students have made their lists, tell them to share with a partner. At this point, students can make changes to their list based on what they learn from their partner.
- Have a class discussion around the items that they chose to bring with them. Start a list and see if the class can reach consensus on 15 items.
- Once you have your list (or not, if you couldn't agree), discuss why it was so hard to come up with a list. Ask students if any other information would have made their decision easier. If the notion of purpose does not come up in discussions (e.g., what I bring to a beach vacation would be very different from what I would bring to a ski vacation), prompt students to think about purpose.
- Give students a specific purpose for their trip and give them a few minutes to change their answers based on the information provided; e.g., on a tropical island, no electricity, lots of edible vegetation, water is available but might not be clean, etc.
- Tell students that the idea of purpose also helps readers decide what information is important to pay attention to and what information is less important. Tell them that, over the next few lessons, you will be practicing how to focus in on important information.

- This activity can be used with slightly different scenarios:

  - Your ship is sinking and you are about to swim ashore to a deserted island. You have time to gather only ten items from the ship. Which ten items would you pick?
  - You just won a $500 shopping spree in a local shopping centre. You have 15 minutes to gather your purchases.
  - There is a computer virus circulating around the planet that is limiting the number of words recognized by computers. Soon, computers will only be able to recognize 50 words. Which 50 words would you choose to still be able to communicate effectively?

Lesson 3 (Guided Practice): Interacting with the Power

In this lesson, small groups of students are assigned a different reading purpose for the same piece of nonfiction.

The focus of this lesson is the importance of knowing your purpose for reading.

- Select a grade-level article that fits with a topic that you have been studying.
- For each group of students, you will need to write a different purpose for reading on a small slip of paper. For example, you could have one group focusing on finding interesting details, another group focusing on finding the cause for an action, and third group focusing on the history of an idea. The focuses for your groups will depend on the type of nonfiction piece you pick.
- Divide your class into small groups of three to four students. Tell students that each group will be making notes about the article they all will be receiving.
- Hand each group their assigned task and a copy of the article.
- Give students time to read the article and complete their assigned task.

I like to have each group record their ideas on large poster paper so that it is easy to share with the class at the end of the activity. Students could also record their notes digitally and use a projector to share it with classmates. They might make use of different note-taking or mind-mapping apps.

- Tell students that they will be participating in a gallery walk to compare the information found by the different groups. Have students rotate around the room to see what is similar and what is different in each group's information. If they are using tablets, each group can quickly share out. Their purpose for reading should not be included or visible on their posters.
- Discuss what students noticed on their gallery walk; i.e., that each group picked out different points of important information.
- Now it is time to reveal the point of the lesson. Select a poster and have that group share what their purpose for reading was. Look at another poster and have that group share their purpose for reading. After the first two, I like to have students try to guess what the focus was for the rest of the posters.
- Finally, have students work independently or in their groups to produce a summary paragraph of the important information based on their assigned task.
- End the lesson by telling students that the reader's purpose for reading helps determine what information is important. Sometimes this purpose is provided for the reader based on the assignment or the questions attached to the reading. Other times, it is up to the reader to provide their own purpose for reading based on the questions that they are wondering about the topic.

Lesson 4: (Guided Practice): Interacting with the Power

In this lesson, students will try to determine the structure of a short piece of nonfiction.

The focus of this lesson is how the author's purpose for writing often affects the structure of the text and helps determine what information is important.

- Choose a grade-level piece of nonfiction text.

For this activity, I like to use a chapter or short section from a textbook.

- Remind students of the preceding lesson and how the reader's purpose for reading affected the importance of certain information. Tell students that, just as the readers' purpose affects how they read a piece of text, the author's purpose for writing affects how the author structures a text.
- Introduce students to the common nonfiction text structures.

Sample List of Common Nonfiction Text Structures

- Cause and Effect: provides reasons or explanations for why or how something happens.
- Compare and Contrast: looks at the similarities and differences between two things. Sometimes presented in the point-by-point method comparing characteristics; sometimes presented in a block method in which one item is discussed and then the other item is discussed.
- Description: outlines the main characteristics of a topic.
- Problem and Solution: describes an issue and provides a way of solving that issue.
- Sequential: provides the order that something happens in.

- Hand out a copy of the text (or an extract from the textbook that you are using). Tell students that their mission is to read the first section of the passage, starting with the heading, and then to read the section of text under the first heading. While they are reading they should try to determine what text structure the author is using. If students have a photocopy, they can write right on the pages; if students have textbooks, they can use sticky notes to record their thinking.
- Read through the first section of the text with the class. Together, see if you can decide what the text structure is. Once you have decided on the structure, mark it down beside the section. You could also have students highlight any key words that helped them determine the structure.
- Work through a few examples as a class and then have students work in pairs to complete the chapter.
- Take a look at the one of the sections that you have worked on as a class. Ask students, based on the structure that you identified, what kind of information is important in the section. Direct students' attention to the idea that text structure helps determine which information is important; for example, if it's a cause and effect structure, the important information will probably consist of an outcome (effect) and a few reasons (causes) for that outcome.
- Finally, have students select one of the sections they have worked on to take notes on. Remind them that the structure will provide clues about what kind of information they should be recording.
- Collect photocopies (or have students transfer their sticky notes to a piece of paper) for formative assessment.

Language for Text Structure

When trying to determine text structure, it is helpful to look for specific transition words in a passage. These words don't guarantee that a passage follows a specific text structure, but they can provide insight into the structure being used.

Cause-and-Effect words: *and then, as a result, in response, consequently, this led to...*

Compare-and-Contrast words: *similarly, likewise, in contrast, on the other hand, whereas*

Description words: *for example, to demonstrate, to illustrate, another*

Problem-and-Solution words: *because, since, for this reason, if...then, the question is*

Sequential words: *first, next, finally, after that, before, then*

Lesson 5: (Independent Practice): Using the Power

The focus of this lesson is using purpose, text structure, and text features to help determine importance.

In this lesson, students apply what they have learned about determining importance by taking quality notes from a piece of nonfiction text.

- Select a grade-level text for students to read.
- Hand out the article. Tell students they will demonstrate their ability to gather important information from a piece of nonfiction text. Provide them with their purpose for reading the article.

Students can use highlighters to identify key text structure words and important text features.

- Remind students that they need to pay attention to both text features and text structure to help them select important information based on the purpose you have given them. As a class, identify the text structure of the article.
- Allow students time to read the article and take notes.
- Once students have finished their notes, have them put away the article. Tell them that they need to write a short summary paragraph of the important information, using only their notes.
- Collect notes for summative assessment.

ASSESSMENT RUBRIC FOR DETERMINING IMPORTANCE

Key

NYM = Not Yet Meeting
M = Meeting
FM = Fully Meeting
EX = Exceeding

	NYM	M	FM	EX
Can locate important information relevant to purpose				
Uses text structure to help locate important information				
Understands the difference between main ideas and supporting details				
Is able to summarize information from text				

Curricular Connection for Determining Importance

All Subjects: Note-Taking

When I first started teaching, I thought that note-taking involved copying down the notes that the teacher provided us. I made it through high school and my undergraduate degree without anyone ever teaching me how to take notes or organize information. Luckily I was able to figure it out, although I am pretty sure that my notes weren't as effective as they could have been.

There are many different ways to take notes and to record information. I like to have a discussion with my students about different forms of notes. I tell them that some people's brains are very linear and find notes that are lined up with the margin, using headings and bullets, most useful. Other people's brains think in terms of connections; notes that are organized in webs showing connections between thoughts are most effective for these people.

Whatever note-taking system works best for each individual, determining important points and linking them together differentiates ineffective from effective note-taking. Good note-takers are able to pull out information that is important to their purpose and organize that information in a way that makes sense to their purpose. They understand the difference between main ideas and supporting details. If your students are taking notes as part of a research project, spend some time explicitly teaching and modeling different note-taking methods.

Sentence Frames to Support Determining Importance

- *The important part of this text is…*
- *The author wants the reader to understand that…*
- *The purpose of this text is…*
- *This text was about _____; more specifically, _____.*
- *The highlights of this text are…*

---

11   Questioning/Inferring

While working on this book, I was speaking about nonfiction reading comprehension with an education assistant who works in one of my classes. We had just finished a lesson on questioning and she commented to me that she was happy that someone was finally teaching students these strategies. She shared her own experience as a student and how she was never asked what she thought about a text, especially nonfiction. In her experience, the only reason to read nonfiction texts was to find a specific piece of information that you were hunting for—a purpose that was usually determined by someone else. She said that when she became an adult, it took her a long time to see nonfiction texts as an opportunity to explore what *she* wanted to know. It took her a long time to unlearn the idea that sometimes you didn't actually have to read nonfiction, you only had to search for the needed information.

Questioning and inferring help move students from being passive readers to being active readers and help drive their thinking forward. Questions and inferences are part of the inner conversation between the reader and the text. If we want our students to think while they read, we need to teach them *how* to have something to think about. We need to teach them to ask their own questions before, during, and after reading. We need to teach them to think beyond the text to infer answers that aren't found directly in the text.

Asking questions before we read helps to prepare our brains to accept new information. These questions connect what we already know to what we are about to learn. They provide a purpose or focus for reading. During reading, we need to ask questions to monitor comprehension and to review content. After reading, we need to ask questions to relate what we have learned to what we already know, and to figure out what we want to learn next.

Teaching students the power to infer teaches them to fill in those *I think...* blanks that teachers love to ask about. Inferring is using clues that are written in the text to fill in, in your head, what is not written in the text. Like fiction inferences, inferences about nonfiction texts must be supported with evidence from the text. Inferences are used to answer the questions in our heads that can't be answered directly by the text.

Questioning and inferring build on the reading powers we have introduced to our students. Many of their questions may arise from previous knowledge they have about a topic. If students do not take the time to reflect on what they already know about a topic, it will be difficult for them to ask questions about how this new knowledge fits in with their previous knowledge. It is important that you continue to model the previous reading powers for students and provide them with additional opportunities to practice these skills.

Sequential Lessons for Questioning and Inferring

Lesson 1 (Teacher-Directed): Introducing the Power

The focus of this lesson is modeling how good readers ask questions before, during, and after reading.

In this lesson, the teacher introduces students to the concept of before-, during-, and after-reading questions.

- Select a piece of nonfiction text that is related to the topic or theme that you are studying.
- If you have already discussed questioning and inferring as part of a fiction unit, remind students about the basics of each of the reading powers. If you have not discussed questioning and inferring with your students, you will need to explain these strategies to students. Tell them that powerful readers ask questions before, during, and after reading to help them understand the text. Powerful readers also try to make educated guesses, or inferences, about questions when they do not find direct answers for them in the text.
- Tell students: *As you read the piece, you are going to share some questions you have about the text or about the topic.*
- Hand each student a copy of the text. Tell them that while you are reading they need to record your questions about the text. If you provide students a photocopy version of the text, they can write your questions directly on the article. If not, they will need to use a separate piece of paper to record your questions.
- Read the title of the article aloud and point out any obvious text features in the piece; e.g., headings or pictures.
- Based on a quick scan of the article, share out any before-reading questions that you have. Try to structure your questions using the frame *I am wondering _____ because of _____*. For example, "I am wondering if the Battle of Midway occurred in the Pacific Ocean because there is a map of the Pacific Ocean on the first page of the article." Try to ask questions around how this new article will fit in with prior knowledge. For example, "I know about a few other battles from WWII, and I wonder where this will fit in with those battles."
- Begin reading the text with students. Pause a few times during reading to continue asking questions.
- Look for opportunities to share a variety of question types with students. For example, try to ask clarifying questions like *It says here that _____, so I am wondering if _____*. Try to ask monitoring-comprehension questions like *I'm not sure what _____ means so I will need to come back to this part.*
- Once you have finished reading the text, share a few after-reading questions with students. Try to ask questions that extend thinking beyond the text. For example: *Now that I've finished reading this text, I am wondering about…*
- End the lesson by having students reflect on their observations: What did you notice about the way I was reading today? What did you notice about the questions I was asking? Did all my questions get answered? How do you think asking questions might help a reader who is reading information? Collect students' lists of your questions for use in the next lesson.

Lesson 2 (Guided Practice): Interacting with the Power

The focus of this lesson is to differentiate between questions that clarify understanding and questions that extend understanding.

In this lesson, students use the teacher's questions from the preceding lesson to decide which questions were answered by the text and which ones require further investigation or inferences.

- Hand students their lists of your questions and the article from the preceding lesson (page 101).
- Tell them that now that you have finished reading the article, you want them to help you sort your questions into two categories: questions that were answered in the text, and questions that were not answered in the text.

You might assign some keener students the task of *answer-finding* to keep them engaged during the discussion. Or try offering questions to the class as a challenge: e.g., *Who would like to try to find out how many different types of sea stars there are?* (See lesson extension below.)

- Write *Answered* and *Not Answered* on the board. Have a student share out one of your questions from the preceding lesson. As a group, decide which heading the question belongs under. If there are students who are unsure if the question was answered in the article, they can take a moment to go back and look.
- Once you have gone through the questions, see if there are any questions for which you can infer answers. Tell students that sometimes we can make inferences based on clues provided in the text or from our own prior knowledge. For example, "I am wondering why the Islands were called Midway. I think it may have something to do with the fact that they are located halfway between Asia and North America."

Extension Activity: Have students research one of your unanswered questions. Give students a short time online or with other resources to find an answer to your question. Students can write you a short letter identifying your question and explaining what they discovered.

- End the lesson by telling students that some of the questions we ask ourselves when reading will be beyond both the text and our own prior knowledge. Encountering these types of questions, the reader must decide if it is something to do more research on, or something the reader can live with not knowing for the time being. If we are left confused, we usually have to go do a bit more reading. If we have a pretty good understanding of the topic for our learning purpose, we may just leave the question unanswered.

Lesson 3 (Guided Practice): Interacting with the Power

The focus of this lesson is using questions to guide our thinking while we read.

In this lesson, students work in groups to create a list of before-, during-, and after-reading questions for a piece of nonfiction text.

- Select a grade-level nonfiction text to read with students.
- Ask students if they remember what types of question you asked during the previous two lessons (questions before, during, and after reading; some questions were answered by the text and some were not).
- Tell students that they are going to practice asking questions before, during, and after reading an article.
- Hand out the text. If possible, project the same text onto a screen or interactive whiteboard. Ask students to divide a piece of paper into three sections with the headings *Before Reading*, *During Reading*, and *After Reading*.
- Read the title of the text and briefly look at any text feature clues; e.g., headings, pictures, etc. Tell students to write a few questions they have before reading the text under *Before Reading*. Remind them that these questions can be based on connections they make, or on things they are wondering about the text.
- Read through the text with students, pausing a few times to allow them time to record their questions under the *During Reading* heading. Use the prompt *What are you wondering so far?* If students seem to be struggling, you can draw their attention to obvious points for questions in the text.
- Once you have finish reading the text, remind students that just because we have stopped reading, doesn't mean we stop thinking! Invite them to write

down a few things that they are still wondering about the topic under the *After Reading* heading.

- Tell students to work with a partner to see which of their questions have been answered by the text. If any question was answered in the text, they can record the answer below the question.
- Finally, have students make an inference about one of the questions they do not yet have an answer to. Remind them that an inference needs to be connected to evidence or prior knowledge and cannot be a random guess. I find it's helpful to encourage students to use the frame *I think* _____ *because* _____ for their inferences.
- End the lesson by discussing how asking questions helped them better understand the text. Collect questions and inferences for formative assessment.

Lesson 4 (Guided Practice): Interacting with the Power

In this lesson, students practice inferring from pictures related to a topic they are studying.

The focus of this lesson is using the clues found in a source to make inferences.

You will need pictures connected to something students already know about, as students need to have background knowledge about a topic in order to make inferences. For example, for a WWI unit, you could show three pictures depicting trench warfare; for an earth science unit, you could show pictures of three different volcanoes.

- Select a series of pictures related to a topic that you are studying. You will need two or three pictures for the class to work on as a group, and then another picture for small groups of students to practice on. If you are not a content-area teacher, select a series of pictures related to a current event.
- Project the first picture so that all students can see it.
- Begin by asking students what they can tell you about the picture. After each answer, ask students, "How do you know that?" If you are projecting on an interactive whiteboard, you can draw lines connecting student inferences to the clue in the picture that prompted the inference. If you can't draw lines, simply record on the board a few words explaining where each inference came from.
- Project the second picture and repeat the process. Continue with all photos.
- Hand out a photocopy of the final picture to small groups of two or three students.

I like to copy the picture on a large piece of paper with lots of white space around it for students to write on. That way, students can record their inferences and connect them directly to text on the photocopy of the picture. If this isn't possible, students can record their inferences on the back of the picture.

- Tell students that it is their turn to come up with inferences as a group. Remind them to include the evidence to support each inference.
- End the lesson by having each group share out a few of their inferences. Discuss how different groups may have come up with different inferences based on their background knowledge. Discuss how examining the photographs added to students' knowledge about the topic being studied. Collect the photocopies for formative assessment.

Lesson 5 (Guided Practice): Interacting with the Power

In this lesson, students practice turning headings into questions and then locating the answers.

The focus of this lesson is using headings from a nonfiction text to locate the answers to our own questions and the questions asked by others.

- Select a grade-level nonfiction text that uses headings to organize information. You can even use your textbook if it is a content-area class.
- Select a short section for students to work with. This section should contain around five headings.
- Hand out the Heading/Question chart on page 107.

See page 107 for the Heading/Question chart.

- Tell students that they are going to use the headings in the text section to create and answer questions.

- Look at the first heading as a class. Ask students what kind of information they think they will find under this heading; for example, under the heading "Weapons of WWII," students will find information about the different weapons that were used in WWII.
- Based on the type of information students think they will find in the section, turn the original heading into a question. For example, "Weapons of WWII" might become "What kind of weapons were used in WWII?"
- Tell students: *Now that we have a question for the first section, we need to check if we came up with the correct question for that heading. We do that by looking for the answer.*
- Read the section with students and try to develop an answer. Tell students that, if they cannot locate an answer for their question, they need to rethink their question, because it probably doesn't match the heading.
- Once you have practiced one heading on your own, have students work in pairs to develop questions and find answers for each of the remaining headings.
- End the lesson by reflecting on the activity with the class: How did paying attention to the headings in the text help you with your comprehension? How did forming questions from the headings help guide your reading? What did you learn today that might help you read nonfiction texts? Collect the chart for formative assessment.

Lesson 6 (Independent Practice): Using the Power

In this lesson, students read a short passage and create a quiz with an answer key for the next reader.

The focus of this lesson is asking quick and deep-thinking questions, and inferring answers for the deep-thinking questions.

- Select a grade-level nonfiction text on a topic you are studying.
- Tell students that they are going to read an article. Once they have read the article, they will be creating a quiz for the next reader. The quiz will need to contain both questions with answers that are found directly in the text and questions that will require the reader to make some inferences. Tell students that you will be assessing their ability to ask quality questions and to infer answers for deep-thinking questions.
- All the questions should focus on important information from the text. Tell students that this is another opportunity for them to practice determining importance.

Depending on your students, you may want to go over some quiz basics:
- writing the quiz on one page with the answer key on the other
- making sure questions are numbered
- allocating a number of marks for each question; i.e., more marks for inferential questions

- Once students have created their quiz and answer sheet, they trade quizzes with a partner. Partners can complete each other's quizzes and then discuss they types of questions that they used.
- Collect quizzes for summative assessment.

ASSESSMENT RUBRIC FOR QUESTIONING AND INFERRING

Key

NYM = Not Yet Meeting
M = Meeting
FM = Fully Meeting
EX = Exceeding

Asking Questions and Inferring	NYM	M	FM	EX
Uses questions to clarify understanding				
Is able to ask questions to extend thinking				
Is able to make inferences based on information from the text and their own background knowledge				
Uses evidence to support inferences				

Curricular Connections for Questioning/Inferring

Science: Scientific Method

I like to equate the idea of questioning and inferring to a simplified version of the scientific method. Students need to ask a question, form a hypothesis (their inference), gather data (support their inference with the text), and communicate their findings.

All Subjects: Answering the Question

For prompts and sentence starters, see page 108 for the Command Terms in Questions chart.

Quite often, students, especially those who are struggling with literacy, fail to answer questions correctly because they aren't sure what the question is asking. I can't tell you how many times I have had to give a poor mark to someone who provided a beautifully written answer containing a lot of information because it answered a question that wasn't being asked. To combat this, include explicit instructions on how to figure out what a question is asking you to do. Teach students the different command terms commonly found in questions (see the chart on page 108). Spending a bit of time defining questions and clarifying what a correct answer would contain helps students more effectively demonstrate their knowledge.

Step 1: Underline the topic or subject of the question (What is the question asking you to comment on?)

Step 2: Circle the command term in the question (What kind of information is the question asking for?)

Step 3: Draw a connecting line between the circle and the underlined word.

SAMPLE FOR ANSWERING THE QUESTION

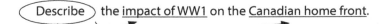

Describe the impact of WW1 on the Canadian home front.

Compare DNA synthesis on the leading and lagging strand.

Sentence Frames to Support Nonfiction Questioning and Inferring

- *What do I already know about...?*
- *What do I wonder about...?*
- *Did this section make sense? Does it fit in with what I already know about...?*
- *What does _____ mean?*
- *When I learned about _____ it made me wonder about _____.*
- *Now that I know _____, I am wondering about _____.*
- *I think _____ because _____.*
- *The part about _____ makes me think _____.*
- *My inference is that _____ because _____.*
- *The author wrote that _____ and that makes me think _____.*

Heading/Question

Heading	Question	Read to find the answer

Command Terms in Questions

If these words are used in the question	In your answer, you need to
Explain *Provide an explanation* *Support* *How* *What causes*	Communicate the important details of an object, event, or sequence of events. Communicate the cause of a certain result
What is the purpose or role	Explain the function, job, or reason.
Illustrate *Outline* *Discuss* *Show* *Describe*	Using words, create a picture of your answer. Clarify by using examples or analogies. Give concrete examples to clarify a point or an idea. Give a description of the main features; summarize the principal parts of a thing, an idea, or an event.
Diagram	Draw a picture that explains the parts and/or operations of something.
When	Explain how long or how soon something happens; your answer will indicate a period of time.
What *Identify* *List* *State* *Suggest*	Provide the name(s) of something based on a set of criteria.
Agree / Disagree *Can*	State your opinion one way or the other; list the reasons for or against. Make a judgment about whether or not something meets the requirements. Your answer will state "yes" or "no" and offer support for that judgment.
Assess	Judge to what degree something meets a certain characteristic and then support your judgment with reasons.
Compare (*Compare* and *Contrast* are often used together)	Describe the similarities between two things.
Contrast (*Compare* and *Contrast* are often used together)	Describe the differences between two things.

12 Transforming

"The ultimate experience in reading is when our thinking changes or is transformed in some way." (Gear, 2008)

To transform means to take the information from your brain, mix it with the information you read, and create a change in thought or knowledge. It differs from a summary in that it is not simply a restatement of the important ideas found in a text. It's a synthesis of the information from the text and the reader's thinking. This "new" knowledge will be slightly different from the old knowledge. It could result in a completely new way of thinking about something, or in a slight change in thinking. Either way, new information can result in a transformed way of thinking for the reader.

Transforming (or synthesizing) is the most complex of the reading strategies, and it requires readers to apply their knowledge of the other four reading powers at the same time. It includes the ability to take information from a variety of sources and compile that information. In order to synthesize information, readers need to summarize information, paraphrase it, and compare and contrast it with what they already know. It requires readers to notice their connections, questions, and inferences. And most of all, to notice these changes, readers need to reflect on their learning.

Because transforming is such a complex idea, it is often confusing for both teachers and students. I find that it is especially difficult to see a true change in thinking after reading only one article about a topic. It is much easier to see a change in thinking after more in-depth study. For that reason, I like to do the guided practice part of this lesson around a series of articles on the same subject.

Another way to make the idea of transforming more concrete for students is to ground your work around a topic under the umbrella of an *essential question*. For example, if you are studying environmental studies, you could use the lens of *How do humans affect the environment?* Students then examine their thinking at the beginning of the unit, during the unit, and at the end of the unit. The answer to the initial big question should transform as they learn.

Transforming Equation:
_____(from my brain)
+ _____ (from the text) = _____(new understanding)

Sample Essential Questions

Social Studies

How is Canada's current government structure similar to or different from those used in Upper and Lower Canada?

What are the causes of oppression?

How does the natural environment influence settlement?

How much impact can an individual have on history?

How much control should governments have over their citizens?

How does where you live affect how you live?

English

How effective is literature in causing social change?

How can literature affect a society's values and beliefs?

How do we form and shape our identities? What makes us who we are?

What is the function of literature in our lives?

Why is it important to tell our story?

How does media shape our view of ourselves and the world?

Why do some prevail over adversity while others fail?

What are the elements of a positive relationship or friendship?

Science

How do living things adapt to their environments?

How do chemical reactions affect our everyday lives?

What causes organisms to change over time?

What causes environments to change over time?

How have simple machines affected the development of civilizations?

How does the motion of the Earth affect our daily lives?

What forces cause changes to the Earth's surface?

Math

How are the four basic number operations related to each other?

Why are graphs helpful?

What tools and units are used to measure various objects?

How do we effectively communicate mathematic equations using words?

Why is the order of operations important?

Sequential Lessons for Transforming

Lesson 1 (Teacher-Directed): Introducing the Power

This lesson focuses on introducing students to the idea that texts can transform our thinking about a topic.

In this lesson, the teacher provides students with an explanation of how a reader's thoughts are transformed by what they read.

- If you have already taught transforming as part of your fiction unit, review the definition of transforming. If your students have not been introduced to transforming, write the term *Transform* on the board. Have students brainstorm a definition for the term. Help them arrive at the idea that transforming means to alter an existing object to create something new.
- Write the term *Synthesize* on the board. Have students brainstorm a definition for the term. Help them arrive at the idea that synthesizing means to combine two things to create something new. (See Transforming lesson for fiction on page 64.)
- Ask students if they see a connection between the two terms (that both terms result in something new being produced).
- Ask students if they have ever been transformed or synthesized. Some might laugh at the idea of being synthesized but many might have examples of how they have transformed over the years.

- Tell students that powerful readers combine the information in the text with the information in their brains to produce new understandings (transformed understanding).
- Finally, tell students that over the next few lessons they will explore how their thinking is transformed by the texts that they read.

Lesson 2 (Guided Reading): Interacting with the Power

In this lesson, students practice selecting passages from a nonfiction text that activate a change in their thinking.

The focus of this lesson is noticing when our brains alert us to new information.

- Select a grade-level text to read with students. Texts that focus on current events are a great choice for this lesson. Students often have prior knowledge and opinions about these events, so examining different perspectives provides an opportunity for their thinking to be transformed. Of course, if you are already focusing on a specific topic in your class, it makes sense to stick with that topic.

See page 115 for the Transforming chart.

- Start by creating a class brainstorm of thinking about the topic; i.e. what you know about the topic as a collective group. Use the Transforming chart on page 115. I like to project the chart onto the whiteboard or interactive whiteboard and fill in the blocks as we work though the process.

Photocopies allow students to write on their own copy of the text.

- Hand out sticky notes so students can record their thinking and place it by the text that triggered the thought.
- Ask students if they ever hear a little voice in their head say "I never knew that" or "Huh, that's new" when they are reading or viewing something. Tell them that this is their brain's way of making them pay attention to new information. This might make them think of connections, questions, or inferences (a reason to practice these other reading powers before this one).
- Tell students that, while you read the article, they need to pay attention to their thinking and "that little voice in their head." Tell them they need to write new ideas on sticky notes and put each sticky note next to the place in the text that triggered that thought. Tell them that you will be stopping to share out your thinking while you are reading.
- Read the article with students, pausing to model your own thinking and to give students time to record their thinking.
- When you have finished reading, ask students to share out their connections, questions, inferences, and new learning around the topic. If you have the chart projected on the board, continue to fill it in as you go.
- Finally, take a look at the list of new thinking that has occurred. As a class, write a summary of how your collective thinking has changed, focusing on new information that students now know and new wonderings or questions that they now have.

Lessons 3–5 (Guided Practice): Interacting with the Power

In this lesson, students track changes to their thinking over time as they read a series of text on the same topic. This lesson will be spread out over three classes.

The purpose of this lesson is to notice how thinking changes as we learn more about a subject.

- Collect a series of three articles or texts about a topic of your choice.

DAY 1

- Tell students that they will be learning about _____ (name the topic) over the next few days. If possible, try to choose a subject they are learning about in one of their content-area classes. Tell them that you really want them to notice how their thinking is changing over the course of the lesson. If you are using the *essential question* model (see page 109), your focus will be on the question rather than the topic in general.

See page 116 for the Three-Article Transforming chart.

- Hand out the Three-Article Transforming chart on page 116. Remind students that it's important to pay attention to what we already know about a subject. Tell students to write down the topic of study in the first row of the chart. Next, have them record any thoughts they already have about that topic in the *First Thoughts* section of the chart. Remind them that some things we are certain about (*I know that…*) and sometimes we are pretty sure that we know something (*I think that…*).
- Hand out copies of the first article. Explain that, while they read the article, students will make note of any important information in the *What the Text Says* column; they will record their thinking around this information in the *What My Brain Thinks* column.
- Collect charts for formative assessment and for use with the next article.

DAY 2

- Hand out student charts from the first day of the lesson. Ask them to take a moment to look back on their original thinking and their thinking around the article presented in the previous lesson. Ask for a few people to share out how their thinking has changed after reading the first article. This will serve as a model for those who are still struggling with the concept.
- Hand out the second article. Remind students that, while you are reading, they need to make note of important information in the *What the Text Says* column and their thinking around that important information in the *What My Brain Thinks* column.
- Collect charts for formative assessment and for use with the next article.

DAY 3

- Begin the lesson by asking students if they remember any of the new thinking they have recorded on their chart; we hope they will feel confident that they can remember what they have written down without a lot of prompting.

Sometimes students are uncomfortable sharing their writing with their classmates. If this is the case, you can remove the names and select a few to share with the class yourself.

- Tell students that you are going to randomly hand out the charts to them today. Each student will take turns sharing out *First Thoughts* column on the chart that they are holding and see if a student claims the chart. If no one claims it, the thinking from the first article is shared out. Continue sharing until all charts have been matched with their original owner. This serves as more modeling for any students who are struggling with transforming.
- Hand out the final article. Since this is the final article in this series, you might choose to let students read this one on their own. You are the best one to judge how your students are progressing with the Transforming power. If you feel they are not ready, continue to read the article with them.
- As with the previous lessons, students make note of important information in one column and their thinking around that important information in the other.
- Once students finish recording their thoughts, have them look back at their thinking over the last three lessons. In the final section of their chart, students write a paragraph about how their thinking has changed.
- Have students share their final paragraph with a partner. If needed, provide students a sentence frame to discuss their thinking (see page 114).

- End the lesson with a discussion of how reflecting on how our thinking has changed helps us learn. Ask students if this was different from other research experiences for which they simply recorded the information without thinking about it.

Lesson 6 (Independent Practice): Using the Power

The focus of this lesson is applying the Transforming strategy.

I like to approve student topics to make sure they are narrow enough to be manageable, but wide enough to allow for a change in thinking.

See page 117 for the Transforming Research chart.

I usually allow two research sessions for this project.

I don't like to call this the end of the journey because, for some students, this will not be the end and they may do more learning about the topic.

In this lesson, students apply what they have learned about transforming their thinking in an authentic learning task that spans multiple days.

- Tell students they are going to embark on a learning journey on a topic of their choosing. For example, rather than studying *Vikings* as a whole, students could focus on one aspect, such as *Viking clothing*. The topic should not be something they already have extensive knowledge about; they need to choose a topic that requires research. If you are using the *essential question* model (see page 109) rather than working with a general topic, students will focus their learning on an essential question.
- Hand out the Transforming Research chart on page 117. Give students time to record their current thinking about the topic. Ask them to record a few questions they are wondering about the topic.
- Tell students they will be allowed to have only the chart and a pen while they are researching. All new information they find needs to be written on the chart.
- After scheduled research sessions, give students time to record their new thinking on the chart. You can remind them of the sentence frames on page 114.
- Tell students they are going to create something to represent their learning journey. They can create a written report, a video, a map—the possibilities are endless.

  1. They need to think back to where they started: i.e., *This is what I thought/ knew at the beginning.*
  2. Then they need to track their journey as they added new knowledge to their minds; i.e., *This is what the texts told me.* Each of their sources should be one of their stops along their journey.
  3. Finally, they need to discuss where they have arrived in their journey; i.e., *This is what I am thinking now.*

- Once students have created a first draft of their learning journey, have them find a partner to share their draft with. Partners can provide feedback to each other.
- End the lesson with a gallery walk, so students can see what their classmates have been working on. Collect learning journeys for summative assessment.

Transformed Thinking	NYM	M	FM	EX
Understands that transformed thinking is a new way of thinking about a topic				
Is able to distinguish between the text and their thinking				
Can provide examples of how information from the text combined with background knowledge to create transformed thinking				
Is able to synthesize information from multiple sources with background knowledge				

Curricular Connection for Transforming

All Subjects: Inquiry-Based Learning

Student inquiry is a great way to incorporate transforming into your classroom. Take a moment to think about all the skills students need to have to conduct a meaningful inquiry: they think about what they already know about a topic in order to decide on an inquiry question; they use more than one source of information; they combine their new learning with their thinking to determine what learning has taken place.

When I talk to teachers about challenges to using inquiry in classrooms, the most common comment is that the students don't seem to have the skills needed to work independently on an inquiry project. I believe that teaching the Reading Power strategies, along with modeling the inquiry process for students, can provide the scaffolding that students need to be successful at inquiring.

Offering free online workshops on a variety of educational topics, thirteen.org has a great one on using inquiry in the classroom. There are also some great books on inquiry mentioned in the Professional Resources list found on page 120. Try *Collaboration and Comprehension* by Harvey and Daniels or any of the *It's All About Thinking* books by Schnellert et al.

Sentence Frames to Support Nonfiction Transforming

- *Originally I thought _____. Now I am thinking _____ because _____.*
- *The part about _____ made me think that _____ because _____.*
- *I used to think _____, but now I think _____ _____ because _____.*

Transforming

Article Title:	Topic:

Our prior knowledge on this topic:

What the Text Says: Quote or paraphrase	What My Brain Thinks: Connections, Questions, Inferences

New thinking on this topic:

Pembroke Publishers © 2016 *Powerful Readers* by Kyla Hadden and Adrienne Gear ISBN 978-1-55138-313-2

Three-Article Transforming

Topic:

First Thoughts about this subject:

Article 1	
What the Text Says:	What My Brain Thinks:

Article 2	
What the Text Says:	What My Brain Thinks:

Article 3	
What the Text Says:	What My Brain Thinks:

In the end, here's how my thinking changed:

Transforming Research

Name:	Topic:
My current thinking on this topic:	
I am wondering	

Source #1	
Important Information:	Bibliography Information:

Source #2	
Important Information:	Bibliography Information:

Source #3	
Important Information:	Bibliography Information:

Now I know
If I were to research this topic more, I would look into

Pembroke Publishers © 2016 *Powerful Readers* by Kyla Hadden and Adrienne Gear ISBN 978-1-55138-313-2

Final Thoughts

Teaching in a secondary-school setting can be isolating. Sometimes we get too wrapped up in our respective subject areas. However, if we seek out opportunities to collaborate with our colleagues, great things can happen. I have learned a lot by working with teachers who have different experience and perspectives from my own. We all have different strengths when it comes to teaching and we need to celebrate and share those strengths.

I truly believe that the two most important things we can do for our students is to teach them literacy skills and to help them become thinkers. I think the two go hand-in-hand. If we want to transform literacy instruction in secondary schools, then we need to

- consider ourselves teachers of reading and thinking, no matter what grade or subject area we teach
- integrate metacognition into all aspects of our practice
- model and demonstrate our thinking for our students, so that they can see what thinking looks like and sounds like
- scaffold our instruction so that we meet students at their level
- provide students with authentic opportunities to read and write every day
- fill our classrooms with quality fiction and nonfiction texts that are accessible to our students
- be passionate readers and show our students how much reading adds to our lives

The important thing to remember about the strategies outlined in this book is that you don't have to change the way you teach or abandon your favorite activities. Reading Power strategies offer you the chance to be more aware of the readers and writers in your classes and to teach them the literacy skills they need to master in order to engage with your subject matter. English teachers, you are probably the literacy experts in your schools, so share that knowledge. Content-area teachers, you really are experts in your fields. Imagine what can happen if your combined your powers!

Happy teaching and learning!

Acknowledgments

I'd like to take this time to acknowledge some of the amazing people that I have crossed paths with in my teaching career. I have the pleasure of teaching in an amazing district that is always open to possibilities. My colleagues are some of the most brilliant educators I have yet to encounter. Early on, I had the pleasure of working with a talented principal named Wendy Woodhurst, who later became our Director of Instruction. From day one, Wendy, you encouraged me to follow my gut, and supported me with professional learning when I didn't know what my gut was telling me. You are the reason I ended up attending a series of workshops with Adrienne and was introduced to Reading Power, even though I was teaching secondary school.

A big thank you to Adrienne Gear for deciding years ago that "we should write a book together." Adrienne, the teaching world is a better place with you in it. The work you do with educators in this province and beyond has affected countless students for the better. Thank you for introducing me to Reading Power and for making sure that the thoughts in my head made sense on paper. Thank you to Mary Macchiusi at Pembroke Publishing for deciding that this idea deserved its own book and to Kat Mototsune for her editing wisdom.

I would also like to celebrate a great little school called Eagle River Secondary in Sicamous, B.C. I really didn't know what I was getting myself into when I applied to teach secondary humanities—I had a moment of panic when I actually got the job! But this amazing school welcomed me with open arms. The administration and teachers, both past and present, are a wealth of knowledge and creativity. It is a pleasure to come to work every day. People don't believe me when I tell them how much laughter happens at my school (even in our staff meetings).

To all my past and present students: you always keep me on my toes. Thank you for being my guinea pigs when I would return from professional learning opportunities. You are the reason I work as hard as I do and am constantly trying to do better. There are too many of you who hold a special place in my heart to mention each of you by name, but I am confident that you know who you are.

To the amazing professors at University of British Columbia, Okanagan: you have broadened my educational vision more than you will ever know. A special thank you to Leyton Schnellert for guidance and wisdom. Leyton, your view of teaching and learning makes my heart sing and my brain do a happy dance. I am eternally grateful for the opportunities you have sent my way. I knew instantly that I had found "my peeps" when I met you.

And thanks, finally, to my friends and family, who support me when I am overly focused on work and welcome me back into their lives when I resurface. Thank you to my parents for teaching me to love reading and for inspiring all of their children to get post-secondary education. Also, thanks to my special someone for being okay with the mountains of books in our house and the constant teacher talk. Over the past two years, you have probably seen more of the back of my laptop than you have of me; yet you continue to support my passion for teaching and learning.

Professional Resources

Allington, Richard (2002) "What I've learned about effective reading instruction from a decade of studying exemplary elementary classroom teachers" *Phi Delta Kappan* 83(10).

Beers, Kaylene (2002) *When Kids Can't Read—What Teachers Can Do: A Guide for Teachers 6–12*. Portsmouth, NH: Heinemann.

Brownlie, Faye (2005) *Grand Conversations, Thoughtful Responses: A Unique Approach to Literature Circles*. Winnipeg, MB: Portage and Main Press.

Brownlie, Faye and Schnellert, Leyton (2009) *It's All About Thinking: Collaborating to Support All Learners in English, Social Studies, and Humanities*. Winnipeg, MB: Portage and Main Press.

Brownlie, Faye, Schnellert, Leyton, and Fullerton, Carole (2011) *It's All About Thinking: Collaboration to Support All Learners in Math and Science*. Winnipeg, MB: Portage and Main Press.

Boushey, Gail and Moser, Joan (2009) *The CAFE Book: Engaging All Students in Daily Literacy Assessment and Instruction*. Portland, ME: Stenhouse.

Duke, Nell and Pearson, David (2002) "Effective Practices for Developing Reading Comprehension" In Alan E. Farstrup & Jay Samuels (Eds). *What Research Has to Say about Reading Instruction*, 3rd Ed. Newark, DE: International Reading Association, Inc.

Gear, Adrienne (2008) *Nonfiction Reading Power: Teaching Students How to Think While They Read All Kinds of Information*. Markham, ON: Pembroke.

Gear, Adrienne (2015) *Reading Power: Teaching Students to Think While They Read*, 2nd Ed. Markham, ON: Pembroke.

Harvey, Stephanie and Goudvis, Anne (2000) *Strategies that Work: Teaching Comprehension for Understanding and Engagement*. Portland, ME: Stenhouse.

Harvey, Stephanie and Goudvis, Anne (2007) *Strategies that Work: Teaching Comprehension for Understanding and Engagement*, 2nd Ed. Portland, ME: Stenhouse.

Harvey, Stephanie (1998) *Nonfiction Matters: Reading, Writing and Research in Grades 3–8*. Portland, ME: Stenhouse.

Harvey, Stephanie and Daniels, Harvey (2015) *Collaboration and Comprehension: Inquiry Circles for Curiosity, Engagement and Understanding*, 2nd Ed. Portsmouth, NH: Heinemann.

Ritchart, Ron, Church, Mark, and Morrison, Karin (2011) *Making Thinking Visible: How to Promote Engagement, Understanding and Independence for All Learners*. San Francisco, CA: Jossey-Bass.

Schnellert, Leyton, Watson, Linda and Widdess, Nicole (2015) *It's All About Thinking: Creating Pathways for All Learners in the Middle Years*. Winnipeg, MB: Portage and Main Press.

Tovani, Cris (2000) *I Read it, But I Don't Get It*. Portland, ME: Stenhouse.

Wilhelm, Jeff (2010) *Fresh Takes on Teaching Literary Elements: How to Teach What Really Matters About Character, Setting, Points of View and Theme.* New York, NY: Scholastic.

Index